The Words that Make Life Work

Daily Self-Talk Messages from the Dean of Positive Self-Talk

Shad Helmstetter, Ph.D., is the author of 17 books in the field of self-talk and personal growth, including *What to Say When You Talk to Your Self,* and *The Power of Neuroplasticity.* His books are published in more than 70 countries worldwide. Shad has appeared on over 1200 radio and television programs, including repeat appearances on Oprah Winfrey, ABC, CBS, NBC, and CNN News.

You are invited to join Self-Talk+Plus™

If you would like to join an online community of positive self-talkers—people like you who are working to make their lives better—you are invited to join Self-Talk+Plus™. This is the inspiring online community where members stream self-talk to their smartphones, get to know each other, join in online activities, receive help from experienced life coaches, and share ideas that help them reach their goals. To visit this amazing online community go to **selftalkplus.com**.

Listen to Certified Self-Talk Programs™ on your tablet or smartphone today at selftalkplus.com.

365 Days of Positive Self-Talk

by Shad Helmstetter, Ph.D.

An Inspirational Guide with Positive Self-Talk Messages for Every Day of the Year

Includes '*Self-Talk Tips*' for Putting Positive Self-Talk to Work in Your Life

Also by Shad Helmstetter, Ph.D.

What to Say When You Talk to Your Self
The Power of Neuroplasticity

365 Days of Positive Self-Talk

Published by Park Avenue Press
362 Gulf Breeze Pkwy., #104
Gulf Breeze, FL 32561
Copyright 2015 by Shad Helmstetter, Ph.D. / All rights reserved

Helmstetter, Shad
    365 Days of Positive Self-Talk

ISBN 978-0-9727821-2-8 *Printed format*
ISBN 978-0-9727821-3-5 *Digital format*

www.selftalkplus.com

Before You Begin . . .

Some starting words to help you
get the most from reading this book,
and *three secrets you need to know.*

The words you say, especially the words you say when you talk to
yourself, not only change your day, they change your life.

This book is based on the amazing scientific discovery that no
matter what age you are, your brain continues to change, and that it
is *always* changing. Because of your brain's neuroplasticity, your
brain is designed to continually rewire itself. And it rewires itself
based on the input it gets. That's why your self-talk is incredibly
important.

Secret #1: The thoughts you think and the words you say
physically and *chemically* change your brain. Your self-talk literally
wires your brain to succeed or fail.

Day after day, word by word, your self-talk is wiring programs
into your brain. And the picture of you that you wire in most is what
you get back out most. *It is your self-talk that creates the foundation for
your success or failure in life.*

Right now, even as you're reading this, you're wiring and
changing your brain.

Your self-talk is the commander of your ship, the director of your life. It is the brain's guiding hand that leads you in the right direction—or in the wrong direction. Your self-talk is the messenger that tells you which path you should follow, what to think and what to do next.

Every thought you think wires your brain to be happy or sad, positive or negative, in a good mood or a bad mood, open to new ideas or closed to them, believing in yourself or not believing in yourself, looking for alternatives or accepting defeat. In fact, everything about you is, at this moment, being influenced or controlled by your self-talk.

What Is Self-Talk and Why Is It So Important?

Self-talk is the direction you give to your brain that tells it how to run your life. Self-talk is everything you say when you talk to yourself. It is your conscious thoughts, and your unconscious thoughts, the thoughts you don't even know you're thinking. It is what you say out loud or what you say silently to yourself. And in its most important form, your self-talk is everything you say or think about *you*—how you feel about yourself—and what you think and what you believe about anything and everything.

Most of us recognize that when we were growing up, we got programmed—and we end up *becoming* those programs and living them out. The remarkable thing, and a great blessing about self-talk, is that you can change that programming. And when you change your programs, you change your life. That's what the *right* self-talk will do for you.

Secret #2: It's been estimated that as much as 77% or more of all of the programs each of us has right now are negative, false, counter-productive, or working against us.

Since it will always be up to each of us to get rid of the negative programs we have, and replace them with the positive kind, any tool that will help us change them can be a blessing. And self-talk is the best tool for changing our programs we have ever found.

In this book you'll find 365 daily self-talk scripts of the right kind of self-talk—the kind of self-talk we should have been getting in the first place. These self-talk scripts are the result of more than 35 years of studying self-talk and how it works, and writing and recording self-talk scripts in dozens of subject areas.

I first began writing self-talk scripts in the late 1970s. At that time, I was studying self-talk and its effects on personal success, and I was writing the first scripts for recording self-talk audio programs for people to listen to. We had learned that with repeated listening, people could permanently wire positive new messages into their brains, just by playing the recorded self-talk in the background.

At the time, the role that self-talk played in people's lives wasn't yet generally understood. Few people realized that their own self-talk, unconsciously repeated throughout each day, was actually programming their brain, and often in the wrong way.

My studies in this field led to the writing of 17 books on the subject of self-talk and personal growth. My first book, *What to Say When You Talk to Your Self*, introduced the subject of self-talk as we know it today. That book is now published in more than 70 countries, and its popularity shows how mainstream the concept of positive self-talk has become.

My recent book, *The Power of Neuroplasticity*, gives the latest updates on this amazing subject, and presents the science behind positive self-talk. It shows clearly that when it comes to its ability to change our lives, self-talk is based on solid science.

Clear, Positive Programs

In *365 Days of Positive Self-Talk*, you'll find daily self-talk messages for reprogramming your brain in a clear, positive way.

The self-talk messages have the power to become much more than a few words you read each day. Reading them, rereading them, and wiring them into your brain could do more than just uplift your year—it could uplift your life.

Reading the self-talk messages one day at a time will give you not only daily inspiration, but also a chance to make each day a better day. However, if you're looking for extra guidance or inspiration at any time, turn to any page to see what you find. If you're looking for an uplift, or need to get back on track, you're sure to find the self-talk you need is just a few pages away.

If you want to get the greatest benefit from this book, read each day's self-talk message as you start your day, and read that same message again just before you go to sleep that night.

There's a reason for doing this that has to do with the way the brain gets programmed. Every time you send a message to your brain, your brain *physically, chemically,* records it temporarily. The more positive messages your brain gets, the more positive directions it will record—and in time, with enough repetition, your brain will go beyond recording them temporarily; it will "wire them in," by creating new neural pathways, and act on them.

Each time you read the positive self-talk phrases in this book, you're sending more healthy messages to your brain. The more you repeat these messages, the stronger and more permanent they become. So you're literally rewiring your own brain with healthy, positive thoughts and messages.

Is Positive Self-Talk Telling You the Truth?

When you first read or listen to positive self-talk, because it's positive and stated in the *present* tense, you might think, *"But that's not me,"* or *"That's not true about me."* That's because some self-talk can sound too good to be true. So is it?

The answer is that positive self-talk paints a new picture of how you're *choosing* to become. It may not sound like you or your life the first time you read it, but it defines the new choices you're making to *become* that way. It may not be you at the moment, but it's a picture of you that you're choosing to create.

The brain listens best to directions that are specific and detailed. The better your brain can see it, the better it can help you create it. That's why self-talk is worded in the *present tense*; to give your brain the clearest, completed picture possible of what you want to accomplish. The clearer the picture you give to your brain of who you want to become, and how you want your life to be, the better your brain will physically 'wire it in' and help you get it.

When you see an artist's illustration of the fabulous new home you're going to build, you don't look at the picture of your home and say, *"This isn't true,"* or *"This isn't real,"* just because your dream home isn't built yet. You look at the illustration of that beautiful new home and see yourself living in it! It may not be a touchable reality when you first imagine it, but it is a future reality in the process of becoming real.

That's what positive self-talk is: *it's a picture of you as you choose to become*—the picture of you you're telling your brain to create. The right self-talk is telling you the truth of who you *really* are, and what you choose to do now to bring the real you to life.

The Most Important Key to 'Success' is
Repetition, Repetition, Repetition

Secret #3: What you repeat frequently, wires the brain. That's so important, it bears repeating: Repetition wires the brain. Because what you experience most, you 'wire in' most, the most important key to success is repetition.

Repetition is the key to wiring or rewiring your brain in the right way because of the way neural networks are formed in the brain. Neural pathways in the brain are formed by repeatedly sending electrical and chemical messages (your thoughts) over the same route—over and over again—like building a highway with layer after layer of concrete or asphalt.

In your brain, each time you travel over the same route—each time your brain receives a repeat of the same message—the pathway becomes stronger and stronger, until, with enough repeated passes, you've created a new 'highway of thought' in your brain.

When similar highways connect, "programs" are formed. These programs—inter-connected mental super highways—become our *beliefs*, our *attitudes*, and our *opinions* about everything. And we create all of them through repetition. Everything we believe, about anything, actually comes to us through repetition. Everything you believe about *yourself*, also comes to you through repetition.

Now, when we want to rewire our brains with better programs, we use the same process. But this time we're repeating better messages—positive self-talk—and building new, more positive, neural networks in the brain.

A message that isn't repeated, only gives your brain a passing thought; it doesn't get wired in permanently. But the exact same message repeated often enough, creates a new neural pathway, and it becomes a 'permanent' part of who you are.

Highlight and Reread Your Favorite Self-Talk

When you find a daily self-talk message that you especially like, or one that speaks to you with special meaning, be sure to mark it so you can easily find it and come back to it.

Since the more often you repeat any self-talk message, the more you'll begin to wire it into your brain, it's a good idea to go back to those messages you'd like to make a permanent part of your positive programs, and read and reread them again.

People often learn to recite lines of their favorite poetry by reading them often. Some of the self-talk you'll find here is poetry for a positive mind, and you can learn and remember it by rereading it frequently.

Also, mark any messages you feel could help you at a later time, should you ever need them. Self-talk messages can offer encouragement, a helping hand, and can uplift your spirit when you need it most.

Reading Self-Talk Out Loud

You'll also benefit from reading the self-talk scripts out loud. When you read aloud you're engaging more senses and increasing your brain activity. When you're reading self-talk out loud and focusing on the message you're reading, you'll increase retention. Reading self-talk in this way isn't required to get the benefit of practicing self-talk, but it will help.

If you find reading aloud is not convenient—you may want privacy when you're reading out loud—or if you find it difficult to add to your schedule each day, just read the self-talk in a normal way, silently, to yourself. The most important thing is to read it, and make it as convenient as possible, so you'll have no reason not to stay with it.

Listening to Self-Talk

Along with reading self-talk each day, you may also want to add listening to self-talk to your daily schedule.

By itself, reading self-talk helps you see each day in a healthy way, and reading even one passage each morning and at night is a habit you should create. When you also listen to self-talk each day, it will help you rewire your brain in a stronger way, and it will do it faster.

Positive self-talk was first written and recorded to be listened to. (The first professionally recorded self-talk programs were introduced in 1981.) The idea proved to be so helpful that many thousands of people now listen to 10- to 20-minute self-talk sessions every day on their smartphones or other listening devices.

Recorded self-talk is different from the self-talk you find in this book. The recorded form of self-talk goes into greater detail; it is more in-depth in specific subject areas that are important to you personally, that you want to work on. In recorded self-talk, each self-talk phrase is also repeated three times, each time with different word emphasis and intonations that increase the strength of the message, and help the brain wire it in faster and stronger.

Recordings of subjects like self-talk for weight-loss, personal relationships, health and fitness, job and career, finances, self-esteem, etc., and even special self-talk for kids and young people, give the listener in-depth self-talk programs that are designed to be listened to each day.

When self-talk is listened to frequently—usually each day for two or three weeks on each subject area you want to work on—the daily repetition of the self-talk causes the brain to rewire itself naturally, and with the right programs. The more often your brain hears those same messages repeated, the stronger and faster they are wired in.

You can listen to all of the recorded self-talk programs that are certified by the Self-Talk Institute at selftalkplus.com.

"Self-Talk+Plus™"

While you're practicing self-talk each day, and you find that the idea of positive self-talk makes sense to you, if you'd like to have more help and support making self-talk a part of your life, and if you'd like to get to know other people who feel the same way, you are invited to join a wonderful community of positive self-talkers at Self-Talk+Plus.

Self-Talk+Plus is an online membership community that was created to bring self-talkers together, give people additional motivation and help, update my readers on the latest news and developments, and stream recorded self-talk audio programs so you can listen to any self-talk you choose at any time, like listening to your favorite online music. You're invited to join us at selftalkplus.com.

"Self-Talk Tips"

Throughout this book you'll also find useful *"Self-Talk Tips"*—helpful ideas and discoveries that will show you how positive self-talk works, where it comes from and what it can do for you.

Instead of waiting to read each *Self-Talk Tip* until you arrive at its place in the book, you may want to skip ahead and read through more of the tips, just as though you're reading a separate "how to" companion book of tips to help you get the most from the daily self-talk messages.

The importance of repetition in creating positive neural pathways in the brain is so important, that some of the key points will be expressed, in different ways, more than once. If you find a key concept idea that is repeated, that's not an accident. That's how the brain gets it, holds it, and, with enough repetition, wires it in.

Enjoy Each Day, and Enjoy the Journey

I hope you'll find the self-talk both uplifting and helpful. And I hope that among the many self-talk messages in these pages, you'll find some of the answers in your quest for the incredible person you were designed to be. To get started, all you have to do is choose a date, go to that page, and let the journey begin.

January 1

"Of all the days I have lived before, of all the days that lie ahead, now is the time to live my dreams, give life to my greatest goals, and live up to the incredible me I was born to be. And the wonderful, positive, promising, and unlimited world I have in front of me, all begins with me, today."

January 2

"Now is a perfect time to get myself in shape. I choose to be healthy and fit, so I eat right, I get the exercise I need, and I make sure I get the right amount of rest and relaxation. And I make sure I give my mind a healthy diet of self-talk that builds my attitude, shows me at my best, and motivates me to reach my goals."

January 3

"Right now l choose to change my life for the better. With every choice l make, l am creating the successes l'm living today, and the future l will be living tomorrow. In everything l do, l choose to find my best."

Self-Talk Tip #1

Positive *Self-Talk* is More
Than Positive *Thinking*

Positive self-talk isn't just about positive thinking; it's about managing *all* of the thoughts that are being wired into your brain.

Unlike basic 'positive thinking'—looking at the world in a generally positive way—positive self-talk could be compared to the flight program the navigator types into the onboard computer on an airplane. Whatever direction the navigator types in is the direction the plane is going to fly. Direction, course, altitude, speed—everything the airplane's onboard computer needs to know to take the plane safely to its destination. It's not just a positive thought or two—*it's a detailed set of program instructions that will fly the plane to its objective.*

Positive thinking, by itself, is a good thing, and it helps you look at the world in a bright and healthy way. But positive self-talk, like the navigator's instructions to the computer, is more specific. The right self-talk identifies every step you need to take to get where you're going, sets the course to get you there, keeps you uplifted and motivated on the journey, and makes sure you arrive safely, and on time.

January 4

"Today I make sure I have focus. When I want to reach a goal, I practice the great success habit of putting all of my attention and energy on one thing at a time. Because I have focus, my thinking is sharp, I see my goal clearly, I stay on target, I take action, and I get it done!"

January 5

"I know that people who achieve, first choose to believe. So I make sure that my attitude is up, positive, optimistic, confident, and going for it! Today especially, I choose to believe in myself, and believe in the winner that I am. I can do it, and I know I can!"

January 6

"I choose to surround myself with greatness: great goals, great supporters, great ideas, great mentors, great self-talk, great vision, great faith, and great belief in myself."

January 7

"Today I get a clear picture of who I want to be. I decide what I need to do to improve myself in some way today, make the choice to do it, and make sure that every choice I make today, will help me become the incredible person I want to be tomorrow."

January 8

"Why do I feel so good about my future? It is because I choose to live with courage, strength, and an unstoppable belief in my ability to imagine the best, overcome challenges, and make things work."

January 9

"Instead of wishing, wanting, waiting, or hoping for things to get better, I make things better, every day. My future is not based on hoping for the best; my future will always be the positive result of how I think, and what I do each day."

Self-Talk Tip #2
Positive Self-Talk Changes the 'Shape' of Your Brain

People who practice thinking positively, physically reshape their brains by changing what they think.

Research has shown that thinking *positively*, physically grows new neurons in the *left* prefrontal cortex of your brain, and boosts your ability to see alternative solutions. That increases your chances of making better choices—and being more successful.

(Tap your forehead above your left eyebrow. That's where a lot of your positive possibilities get their start. The correct self-talk grows more neurons there.)

Meanwhile, people who think *negatively* grow more neurons in the *right* prefrontal cortex of their brains. That causes them to close off opportunities and ideas that could have helped them succeed. When you're thinking negatively, your brain is also processing potential solutions at a slower rate. Why? Because it's busy dealing with fright, fight, or flight, instead of focusing on the positive solutions that could have solved the problem.

If your self-talk is positive, you're not only wiring in new neural pathways that change how you feel, how you look at life, and how successful you're going to be at just about anything; you're changing the structure of your brain in the right way.

January 10

"It's not what has happened in the past that matters, it's how I rise above it that counts. It's not about what I've gone through or endured; it's what I choose to do next that creates the incredible life I have in front of me."

January 11

"It all gets down to what I believe about me. If I think I can do it, I can. If I believe I have it, I've got it. If I really want it, I go for it! If I truly believe in me, I'll prove it!"

January 12

"I see change as a natural part of life, the next pathway to my positive future, and the opportunity to grow. In any change that comes my way, I look for the opportunity in the change, I find a way to learn and grow because of it, and I make it work"

January 13

"When it comes to my goals and my dreams, I let nothing or no one take them from me. I hold the key that opens the door to my own unlimited future. That future is mine. What I do with it is up to me."

January 14

"A perfect description of me would include the words *positive, strong, sincere, kind, caring, believing, goal-oriented, intelligent, energetic, full of life, and determined to live up to my best.* That's me. That's the person I choose to become. That's the way I was born to be."

January 15

"I choose to dream, to believe in, and to create, the most remarkable, positive future for my world and for the life I'm living. I may be practical and down to earth in most things that I do, but when it comes to creating my own future, I also choose to dream, and I'm always willing to believe in the best."

Self-Talk Tip #3
Seeing the Glass as Half *Full*

Behavioral researchers have shown that when it comes to your goals, you only reach what you can see. Or, put another way, you only reach the goals you can clearly imagine. That's true of the biggest and the smallest things in life. Overall, if your brain can't 'see it,' you probably won't get it.

The 'glass' is, of course, a metaphor for what we believe or what we imagine to be. Since the brain will work hardest at helping you get those things that you can most clearly imagine, if your glass is 'half empty' and you can't see the possibility of getting what you want, your brain won't help you get it—*you're wiring your brain to believe it won't work.*

Seeing the glass as half empty stops you from seeing the opportunities that are in front of you, and programs your brain to act as though you won't get what you want. The result is, you usually won't.

When you practice seeing the glass as half full, you literally switch on the part of your brain that searches for alternatives and possibilities. So instead of your brain being busy being negative—and making sure something won't work—when you change your brain to think in the positive, it gets busy looking for ways to make it happen.

January 16

"I choose to have an incredible day! Positive and good in every way. My attitude starts with the words I say, and I choose to have an incredible day."

January 17

"I take time for me. I know that my life works best when I set aside time that is just for me, so I plan it, and I do it. I make sure that I am strong in spirit, well-rested, have peace of mind, and feel good about myself. To do that, I take time for me."

January 18

"Right now is a great time to make the choice, gather my energy, fine-tune my focus, get a clear picture of what I want to accomplish, decide to do it, smile, say *yes!* to myself, take a deep breath, and go for it!"

January 19

"My day today is up to me! So l choose to fill my day with high energy, have a great attitude, know that things are going right, and create a positive outcome in everything l do. My day today is up to me, and l choose to make today an incredible day!"

January 20

"I never let problems or challenges hold me back or stop me. Instead of letting problems get me down, I keep myself up! I keep my eye on the goal, take the right action, believe in the best, have faith, move on, and make my day a winning day."

January 21

"I don't need someone to give me my success, or to do it for me. All I need is a dream I believe in, a goal to achieve it, the enthusiasm to give it life, the decision to take action, and the determination to make it happen, and I will create my success from my dream."

Self-Talk Tip #4
You Were Born to be Successful

Negative self-talk tells us that we deserve *less* than the best. When it comes to love, money, talents, skills, luck, job promotions, good looks or almost anything we'd *like* to have, but may not think we can get, it's our own negative self-talk that's telling us what we don't deserve.

The truth is a different story. You were born to succeed. All of us were. No exceptions. You were designed to excel. Like the flowers of the field or the birds in the sky, one is not created to succeed while another is created to fail. When it comes to life itself, we were designed in every way to grow, learn, overcome challenges, become stronger, and reach the highest levels of personal growth and fulfillment. That's true of all of us.

Blessings aren't handed out randomly or unfairly—more for some and fewer for others. Blessings are given out in direct proportion to *our intention of receiving them, our willingness to work for them, and our willingness to believe in them.*

The real you, the true you that you were born to be, deserves every blessing you choose to imagine and accept. And that gets down to your self-talk and your beliefs about yourself. You will accept and create what you believe you deserve.

Check your self-talk. Make sure you've got the right programs of self-worth and deserving. When it comes to how much you deserve, no matter where you've been or what has happened in your life so far, you were born to have an equal share in the universe. You still have it.

January 22

"I don't wait for success to just 'happen,' or quietly 'hope' for good fortune to come my way. When it comes to my success, I choose it, I create it, I go for it, and I make it happen."

January 23

"I never let the problems, troubles, or unrest in the world we live in get me down. Every day I keep my focus, work on my goals, and believe in the best outcome in everything I do. I make sure my attitude is always up, look for the bright, and find the good."

January 24

"Today I choose to have a great attitude! How I feel about today, and what I do with it, is really up to me. So I choose, right now, to have an incredibly good attitude, feel great about myself, decide to go for it, and make today one of my best days ever!"

January 25

"I am not alone. I have my life, my dreams, my goals, and my determination to succeed. And I make sure I always surround myself with my undying faith, others who believe in me, and an unstoppable belief in myself."

January 26

"I have vision. Every day I practice seeing 'the big picture' —how life works, and what I can do now to make my life work best. So I choose to have vision. I see the future I'm creating, and I see a future that works."

January 27

"I know the great truth: that my life, and what I do with it each day, is up to me. I know that I alone am responsible for what I think, what I do, and what I say, and I practice being in control of my life every day, in every positive way."

Self-Talk Tip #5
Self-Talk in Sports

Self-talk can help you in virtually any area of your life. But a good way to measure the results is in studies with athletes.

As just one example, a study of the use of self-talk in a cycling competition showed an *18%* increase in endurance among bicyclists who practiced self-talk techniques for two weeks prior to the event. *Eighteen percent* is a dramatic and game-changing increase, when even a 2% increase in endurance can win the race.

In the test, the control group, which used self-talk only during the tests, with no previous self-talk practice, had *no* increase in endurance. Meanwhile, the members of the group who practiced self-talk two weeks in advance were literally *rewiring their brains* to create more endurance during the race.

As science is repeatedly showing us, self-talk, when used correctly, is an effective tool that can wire new, helpful, neuron pathways in the brain. If practicing the right self-talk can give you that great an edge in sports, imagine what it can do in the rest of your life.

January 28

"I take time to improve myself, and I work at getting better at anything I do. I may be doing okay so far, but just watch me. Because I'm working at improving myself in some way every day, I will become even better tomorrow."

January 29

"Every day I look for the good, and every day I find it! I find it in my family, in my work, in my friendships, in my thoughts, in my goals, in my future, in the world around me, and always in myself. Every day I look for the good . . . and I find it!"

January 30

"I will not be stopped when other people doubt me. I will not be held back by other people's fears. I have my goal; they have theirs. I have a road that is mine to follow, and I choose to believe in myself, follow my path, and keep going. And because I do, I will reach my goals, and I will win."

January 31

"Today is a great day to help others succeed. I care about others, and it shows. I choose to help people get better, in any way I can. And when I help others do better, my life gets better, too."

Self-Talk Tip #6
Reading Self-Talk Every Day, *Resets* Your Brain in a Positive Way

Reading positive self-talk every day does three important things for you:

#1. Adding the right self-talk to your day sets up your brain in a neurologically *healthy* way. When you practice positive self-talk, you tell your brain to think that way throughout the day. Doing that resets your focus, and that makes your brain work to make each day more positive.

#2. Reading daily self-talk opens your mind to positive new ideas that the self-talk messages inspire. The practice of reading self-talk will help you create the habit of attracting positive new thoughts, and through repetition, begin to create new programs. That makes you more aware of what's going on in your life, and ready to take action in the right direction.

#3. Reading daily self-talk gives you an immediate attitude adjustment. The more positive your self-talk, the better the day you're likely to have. Your self-talk directs your attitude, and your attitude directs your day. If you want to have more good days, start and end each of them with positive self-talk.

February 1

"Today I'm going for it! I know my goal, I know what I want to do, and I know that all I have to do is do it. So I choose to take control of my day, stop the excuses, put myself into motion, take action, put all of my energy into making it work, and refuse to stop until I reach the goal."

February 2

"Every day I choose to make the best of any situation. No matter what, I practice having a winning attitude, a 'can-do' spirit, and a non-stop belief in making things work. And what does practicing having a great attitude do for my life? It makes it better in every way."

February 3

"I make the time to spend my time with people who are upbeat, positive, and going for it! The more I surround myself with people who succeed, the more positive I am, the more I learn, the better I do, and the more successful I become!"

February 4

"I never wait for someone else to lift me up, set my course, or get me moving. I know that my success is up to me. What I believe, is what I achieve. And every day I choose to believe in the best and create my success."

February 5

"I choose to be healthy in every way. I choose to eat right, get the nutrition I need, rest well, exercise often, be productive, look for the good, avoid negative people, avoid negative habits, help others, always think in a positive way, smile a lot, believe in the best, and always picture myself and my future, living a life of health and success!"

February 6

"It's not 'luck' that makes my life work; it's how I look at it. I choose to see the bright, find the good, believe in a positive outcome, and always have faith that I will overcome the challenges and succeed. And because that's how I choose to look at my life every day, time after time, I win!"

Self-Talk Tip #7
From *Self-Talk* to *Success* in 5 Steps

One of the subjects the book *What to Say When You Talk to Your Self* discusses in detail is the process by which changing your self-talk leads to actual changes that take place in your real life. Here it is in a nutshell:

1. When you change your self-talk, you change what you *believe* about yourself.
2. When you change what you believe about yourself, you change your *attitude*.
3. When you change your attitude, you change your *feelings*.
4. When you change your feelings, you change your *actions*.
5. When you change your actions, you change your *results*.

To test this for yourself, think of something in your life (or in yourself) you'd like to improve. Then focus on that area of your self-talk for two or three weeks. When it comes to that subject, give it your full attention, and completely change *all* of your self-talk about that subject—to the positive.

When you do that, and stay with it, you will change your belief, your attitude, your feelings, your actions, and your results.

February 7

"Today I choose to focus on my goals, get a clear picture of what I need to do next, make the decision to take action, get my attitude in shape, put myself into motion, and make today a get-it-done day!"

February 8

"I am always mindful of being mindful. I am consciously aware of being aware. Because I'm mindful, I listen to what I say, and I also listen carefully to my thoughts. Because I'm mindful, I'm in control of what I think, what I say, and how I feel."

February 9

"I choose to see my own future as a bright, positive, healthy, exciting place to be. That's the future I choose to live. And today and every day, in everything I do, that's the future I choose to create."

February 10

"When it comes to my attitude, I'm up! When it comes to my goal, I'm going for it! When it comes to staying with it, I'm there! And when it comes to making my day an incredible day, I'm on it, I've got it, and I'm making it happen!"

February 11

"When I change my Self-Talk, I change what I believe about myself. When I change what I believe about myself, I change my attitude. When I change my attitude, I change my feelings. When I change my feelings, I change my actions. And when I take the right actions, I create my success."

February 12

"When I have doubt, I choose to have faith and believe in the best. When I feel I just can't win, I refuse to give up or give in. When I'm not sure about my purpose in life, I remind myself that I'm here for a reason. And when I wonder whether I can go on, I always choose to take one more step forward."

Self-Talk Tip #8
Tying a String Around Your Finger

Before the days of smartphones and smart watches, people sometimes tied a string around their finger to remind them of something important they wanted to remember during the day. Reading daily positive self-talk messages is a similar kind of reminder.

Each self-talk message you read each day not only gives you a positive perspective on the day, it also reminds you that every thought you think that day, is important. The more days you focus on that one idea—*that your thoughts wire and change your brain*—the more mindful and aware of your thoughts you'll become. And the more mindful you are, the more you take control of your thoughts, your life, your direction, and your destiny. That makes a small daily reminder a very big thing.

February 13

"Of all the people who help me, influence me, or guide me in any way, the one person who has the most control over my thoughts, my actions, and the direction of my life is the person I spend the most time with each day. The one person who holds the key to who I am and who I will be, is me."

February 14

"I choose to live in the present. Because I focus on the 'now,' I am alive, aware, and completely in touch with the life I am living. This day, this time, and this moment are a gift to me, and I choose to live this gift to the fullest."

February 15

"I practice my 'people skills' every day. I pay attention. I listen. I always build up and never tear down. I look for the good and I find it. I'm helpful, caring, supportive, and encouraging. I believe in people and I let them know it. I care about others, and it shows."

February 16

"I have been given the incredible gift of being me.
So I choose to live up to the promise only I can fulfill.
I have so much to discover, and so much to live; so
much to offer, and so much to give. And every day
I choose to live up to my best, and to become the
me I was created to be."

February 17

"I do my best when I feel good about myself, and how I feel
about myself is always up to me. So right now I take a good
look at the real me, and choose to like who I see. I can always
get better, but I like who I am and I'm glad to be me."

February 18

"I am a person of exceptional quality. I have skills,
talents, abilities, and potentials that make me special in
so many ways. That is the real me as I was intended to
be. How do I know? That's the way God made me in
the first place, and God makes winners, not mistakes."

Self-Talk Tip #9
How Self-Talk Works

Your brain needs a lot of healthy programs in order for you to succeed or do well in life. Self-talk is a way for you to get positive new programs wired into your brain. It's based on neuroscience—on how the brain works—but it isn't hard to understand:

Your brain records every message you give it. The part of the brain that records those messages doesn't know the difference between something that is *true,* and something that is *false.* Positive or negative, bad or good, your brain just records it, and then acts on it. Any message you send to your brain *repeatedly* (by reading, speaking, or listening) gets wired in, and your brain acts on it as though it's *true*—whether or not it was true to begin with.

Giving your brain the right self-talk messages physically wires your brain with positive, new neural pathways that in time become the new you —but with better programs. Your day-to-day success is based on the number of positive neural pathways that get wired in.

The more you practice using the right self-talk, the more healthy, new neural pathways you wire into your brain.

February 19

"I make sure that every goal I set, and anything I plan to accomplish, is not only of benefit to me; it will also be a force of good in the lives of anyone else it touches."

February 20

"I don't mind it when others question my goals or think I can't reach them. I know that real winners win by following their greatest dreams, rather than listening to the negative opinions of others. So I don't give up, and I don't give in. And because I keep believing in myself, I win!"

February 21

"I practice living each day in a peaceful, calm, and mindful way. The reason I do that is because it's a healthy, mature, and intelligent way to live—and it makes every day better."

February 22

"I can't wait to greet the day each morning. I have so many goals, dreams, and possibilities in front of me, and I choose to make my dreams come true. So every day I wake up, think up, get up, and go for it!"

February 23

"I never allow other people's doubts, criticism, or lack of vision, to stand in my way. I choose, instead, to set my own course, follow my own path, believe in myself, have my own vision, and make every day an incredible day."

February 24

"I alone choose every thought I think. I alone am responsible for the direction of my day. I may be surrounded by the love, help, and support of others. But I alone must choose my path, and I alone will find my way."

Self-Talk Tip #10
The Right Self-Talk is also
Practical Self-Talk

The right kind of self-talk is positive, but it's also practical. Positive self-talk helps you see the world in a brighter way, but it also makes sure you are realistic, clear-minded and level-headed. With the right self-talk, you don't ignore problems or challenges—you deal with them. You don't pretend everything is rosy; you see life for what it is, but you're better equipped to handle it.

When you read the self-talk on these pages each day, at first glance it could seem like the picture of life the self-talk shows you, is too good to be true.

But read on. You'll also find self-talk that sounds something like an internal drill sergeant; it tells you to knuckle down, be responsible, work hard, take action, do it now, stop complaining, keep going, and refuse to quit. Great self-talk, and very practical.

February 25

"I refuse to worry, or let the challenges of the moment, or the problems of the day get me down. I'm here, I'm alive, I'm alert, I'm awake, and aware, and I'm ready to make today a successful day in every way!"

February 26

"I choose to live my life by choice, not by chance. My success each day, each hour and each moment, is not up to luck or fortune; it is up to the choices I make. And because I choose success, I choose to make good choices."

———

February 27

"Changing my life for the better, by thinking right, thinking up, and choosing to succeed, always works best with practice. So I practice looking at life in the most positive possible way, every day. And the more I practice, the better I get."

February 28

"l am attractive in many ways. l attract others to me. l attract their interest, l attract their positive attention, l attract their friendship, and l attract their belief. l attract the very best in everyone. Therefore, l am attractive!"

February 29 (For Leap Year)

"Sometimes, when my dreams are high enough, and the challenges are big enough, it takes a leap of faith to get me there. But I have my plan, I know the goal, I take the leap, and I get there."

Self-Talk Tip #11
You Deserve the Credit
For Your Success

Because of the power of neuroplasticity—your brain's ability to continually change itself—who you become and how successful you'll be, will be less up to your upbringing or the circumstances of your life, and more up to the wiring you decide to create *next* in your own brain. At least it can be.

When you practice the right self-talk, you grow new neural pathways and create new connections in your brain. Everything you think and everything you do is based on the strongest of those neural connections.

Since those connections are created by the self-talk *you* decide to practice most, you are the one who is actually creating your own success. So when it gets down to it, *you're* the one who gets the credit for your success. You're the one who decided to program your brain in a positive way, change your wiring, and create your success. Congratulations!

March 1

"I know that loss, and losing someone or something very important in my life, can seem unfair in every way. So I choose to do my best to accept the truth of my loss, continue to trust in a brighter, more sensible day to come, have the patience to wait for the sunrise, and believe with all my heart that the light is coming."

March 2

"Why do I wait for something better? Why would I put off my future, when I can start right now? Today I choose to take control of my life, decide what I want to do next, set my goals, put myself into action, and take a clear, positive step *up* into my own, unlimited future."

March 3

"I make choices that keep me fit. I eat right, and I feel good about taking great care of myself. I know that my fitness starts with my attitude, so I make sure my attitude about my diet and the food I eat is healthy and positive, and always helps me live up to my best."

March 4

"I manage my thoughts, my feelings, what I do, and what I say. I never get angry for any wrong reason, and I'm always in control of myself. I am mature, experienced in life, very thoughtful, considerate of others, and I choose to be in control of who I am, how I feel, and everything I say and do."

March 5

"I have patience. I understand that some things take time. When I need to get something done, I do it, but when I have to wait for time to run its course, I consciously take the time to understand, wait with an attitude of calm and quiet, and appreciate the opportunity to watch my world work."

March 6

"I pay attention. I am aware of being aware. I see and hear things that other people may never notice. And in every moment, I am aware of the moment I'm in. I'm aware of everything important around me, what's happening, and why, and how I can live this moment in my life in the most aware, awake, and alive way."

Self-Talk Tip #12
Clearing Out Your 'Mental Apartment'

Imagine that you live in a "mental apartment." You've had the same old furniture for years. (The "furniture" is your old mental programs.) You got your hand-me-down furniture—your old way of thinking—from your family, parents, teachers, friends, and all of your past. It's old furniture. It's tattered and worn, but you're used to it, and it's all you know—it's your old way of thinking.

Now let's say you want to clear out your mental apartment, so you decide to get rid of all of your old mental furniture by getting rid of all of your old negative mental programs. So you take all of that old furniture out and store it out of sight in your garage.

The next morning you wake up to a beautifully empty mental apartment. No old negative furniture. No old easy chair of negative opinions. No old desk with drawers full of bad attitudes. No old television set spewing out negative programs. Your mental apartment is completely empty, and you realize you have nowhere to sit or do anything.

So what do you do next? After a while you go out to the garage and start bringing the *old* furniture back in! First you bring back in that old easy chair of "negative opinions"—the one you were going to get rid of. And then, later the same day, you bring in the old desk. That night, you bring back in the old television set. Finally, after just a day or two, your entire mental apartment is filled back up with the same old, tattered, *negative* furniture that you were used to living with. Why did you bring it all back in? *Because you didn't have any new furniture to replace it with.*

If you want to get rid of the old negative furniture in your life, you have to replace it with something better. You have to get new positive "furniture"—new programs—or your *old* programs will come back in!

The new furniture is your new self-talk. Positive self-talk replaces the old negative furniture in your mental apartment with new, positive programs. When you learn the new self-talk, you change the furniture in your mental apartment for good. And that's the beginning of changing your life.

From *What to Say When You Talk to Your Self* by Shad Helmstetter, Ph.D.

March 7

"I refuse to ever let unnecessary worry or fear rule my life. I'm strong, I'll get through it, I'll get past it, and I'll be better because of it. Any time I feel worries or fears tugging at my mind, I immediately give myself the self-talk that says, 'I'm up to this, I can do this, I'm strong, I'm capable, I'm bigger than the problem, and this too shall pass.'"

March 8

"I like to smile and I love to laugh. I make sure that every day is a day that is filled with joy, laughter, happiness, and feeling good about being alive and being me, in every positive way. I know that happiness is a habit and a way of life, and I make sure my own happiness is a part of every day I live."

March 9

"I don't just stop and smell the roses. Every day, day after day, I stop and appreciate my life. I always remember that every day I live is a day filled with countless blessings, endless hope, and unlimited promise. Just to be here and to be me is an incredible blessing, and I know it and I show it every day."

March 10

"I am more than I could have ever imagined. I am responsible, and I always take care of my work and the day-to-day obligations of my life. But there is more to me than my work, or the daily details of my life. My possibilities are endless, my future is unlimited, and I always take the time to remember that I was also designed to soar with the eagles."

March 11

"Money may be essential, and having enough is important. But wealth, to me, is more than dollars and material possessions. I choose to measure my life not by how much I can posses, but by who I am as a person, what I'm doing with my gifts, and how much I'm helping others."

March 12

"I will never stop seeking and learning. I choose to listen, study, find new interests, always be curious, keep an open mind, correct myself, learn new things, keep on growing, and never stop. As long as I am here, I will not only excel, I will truly live."

Self-Talk Tip #13
Does "Thinking Positive" Really Make Things Better?

Does creating more "positive" neural pathways in your brain improve your life?

Not everyone who practices positive thinking immediately experiences sudden success in every area of their lives. But it's clear that, along with being generally happier and more upbeat, people who think more positively—as a way of life—experience the results of their positive attitudes in ways they never expected.

When your brain is working for you instead of against you, it can help you in ways you might never have thought about. A positive thinking brain literally opens new doors and new chances that are closed to the person who thinks negatively.

According to research in neuroscience, the most significant reason positive thinkers do better overall is that by wiring your brain to be more positive, you open your brain to alternative solutions—you don't sell yourself short by quitting when a problem comes up. You refuse to quit before you find the solution that works. And you gain an attitude that helps you succeed.

The doorways to alternative solutions are available to everyone, but they're most visible to people who practice thinking positively. Positive thinkers see more of those doorways because they have literally rewired their brains to search for solutions—instead of dwelling on the fear of failure.

March 13

"I choose to practice the incredible art and skill of day dreaming. I get rid of the limits; go beyond the boundaries; and in my mind, fly to the farthest reaches of my imagination. When I'm dreaming of the endless universe of potential that surrounds me, I am wiring my brain to take me there."

March 14

"I choose to be happy. I know that being happy, day by day, is a choice. And because happiness is also physically healthy, attitude-adjusting, mood-elevating, emotionally stabilizing, success-generating, immediately uplifting, day-changing, and contagious, I choose to be happy."

March 15

"I refuse to let set-backs or disappointments get me down. That's life, and life is exactly as good as I choose to make it. So I choose to see life in the most positive, optimistic way. I always deal with the challenges of today, but I never forget the unlimited possibilities of tomorrow."

March 16

"I choose to live a life that adds to the lives of others. I believe in, care about, uplift, support, and encourage others. Living in service to the lives of others adds value, purpose, and meaning to my life every day."

March 17

"I think twice. If someone says something to me that I could take the wrong way, I think twice. When I hear something that could anger or upset me, I think twice. And when I see someone I disapprove of for no apparent reason, I think twice. Before I allow myself to think 'negative' about anyone at any time, I think twice."

March 18

"I choose my work and I enjoy what I do. I choose to make each workday important, positive, and productive. Through my work, I practice and improve my skills and abilities, I help take care of my family and home, I create service to others, and I find fulfillment that is rewarding in many positive ways."

Self-Talk Tip #14
Three Steps to Changing
Your Programs

Your brain is built to constantly wire and rewire itself with new information; it is designed to change its programs if you tell it what to do. There are three steps you can take that will help you do that.

Step 1 – *Monitor*. Monitor means to listen to everything you say when you're talking to someone *else*, everything you say when you're talking to *yourself*, and even the thoughts you *think*. Consciously listen to everything you say or think.

Step 2 – *Edit*. You have the ability to edit and change anything you are about to say, or anything you're about to think. If what you were going to say or think next is actually negative self-talk, *don't say it. Don't think it*. Change it. Turn it around. Get it right. Turn it into a positive.

Step 3 – *Listen*. The best way to change old programs rapidly is by listening to new self-talk. It was by hearing the messages that were spoken to us originally that we received most of our old programming; it is by hearing the *right* self-talk repeated that those old programs are most easily changed.

People now listen to recorded self-talk sessions that are streamed to their tablets or smartphones. When you listen in this way, it's like learning a new language—by listening to it repeatedly until it gets wired in.

Self-talk programs to listen to on your smartphone or listening device are available at selftalkplus.com.

March 19

"When I go to work, I make the choice to make it a good day. I look forward to my work, and I perform my responsibilities with enthusiasm. I make each work day a good day. Because how I feel about my work is up to me, I make it positive in every way."

March 20

"When something happens that gets me down, I make sure that I always get back up. I know that life happens, and not every day can be like I'd like it to be, but that doesn't bother me. I make sure my attitude is up, bright, and positive, and ready for the possibilities of the next day to come."

March 21

"I practice being level, stable, and strong. I don't let everyday problems throw me or upset my day. When I face a problem, I deal with it and go on living. That's just life, and I love life and I'm glad to be here!"

March 22

"I practice having a happy, positive mind. The more optimistic I am, the more I train and prepare my brain for success. The more positive I see my life, the more opportunities come my way, the more doors are open to me, the more I grow, and the more peace of mind and happiness I create."

March 23

"I could see each day and the world around me as down, negative, filled with problems, and nothing but obstacles and stress. But I choose, instead, to see each day as an incredible gift—a positive opportunity to live up to my best, get better every day, and be thankful for the chance to go for it."

March 24

"I refuse to measure my life by comparing myself to anyone else. I am living my life for my reasons, my purpose, and my destiny, not theirs. My goal is not to be as good as someone else; my goal is to be as good as I was created to be."

Self-Talk Tip #15

Why Do *Negative* People Think *Positive* Thinking Doesn't Work?

Negative people often see life as difficult and filled with problems, and tell themselves that positive thinking doesn't work.

When people see life as dark or difficult, they typically do so because their brains have become physically *wired* to see it that way. They can't see the benefits of being optimistic because their brains are wired to focus on the negative, and they seldom experience what true optimism feels like. So to them, life *is* negative, and because their brains are programmed that way, that's what they see.

Every input each of us gets repeatedly, physically wires our brains with positive, neutral, or negative programs—and most people who end up with negative wiring have no idea their wiring is negative or working against them. It's not their fault, of course; it's their programs. (If you know someone like that, give them this book.)

March 25

"I listen to my regular, everyday voice. But I also listen carefully to the voice that is the higher, wiser part of me. To hear my wiser, inner voice, I make sure that I take the time, find the quiet, go within, be patient, and listen carefully. And the more I listen, the better my life works."

March 26

"When something goes wrong, or when I'm very disappointed, instead of thinking that life is against me, I choose to think about what is *right* with my life. I always find that when I add things up, there is far more positive than negative; life is working; and if I want things to go my way, it's up to my attitude, and up to me."

March 27

"I choose to be alive, alert, and aware. I am endlessly curious, interested in new things, always ready to learn, and getting smarter every day. I'm not just hoping or wishing I could improve who I am. I'm practicing personal growth every day, and it's working."

March 28

"I know that the path I choose to take in life is mine to find and mine to follow. I may have guidance and support along the way, and some of my steps may ask for the help and belief of others, but the path I follow is mine to choose and up to me."

March 29

"I am an active thinker, and never a lazy thinker. Instead of letting my mind drift aimlessly from thought to thought, I practice being consciously aware of every thought I think. With practice, I not only become more mindful of my own thoughts, I choose thoughts that are clear, lead me forward, and improve my life."

March 30

"I am trustworthy and reliable. Other people can count on me, and I can count on myself. What I say I will do, I do. I make sure I do not over commit, and I always keep the commitments I agree to. Being reliable and worthy of trust is a choice, and it is a choice I have made. I am trustworthy and reliable."

Self-Talk Tip #16
Watching For the
Saber-Toothed Tiger

People who habitually think in a negative way spend more time activating the "amygdala" part of their brain than people who think in the positive. The amygdala is the *"Danger Will Robinson!"* part of the brain, and one of its jobs is to warn us when we're threatened in any way.

The amygdala got that way when it was trying to keep us safe from saber-toothed tigers. It hasn't yet learned that we no longer have to sit up nights to keep the campfires going and watch for saber-toothed tigers.

It's good that our brain has a built-in early warning system to help keep us safe, of course. But when we spend too much time listening to messages from the amygdala, our brain gets wired with the notion that we're always in peril, and we react accordingly.

That's where too much fear, doubt, disbelief, lack of hope, and despair all come from—not knowing when to stop listening to an overactive amygdala. And in time, listening to that doubt, uncertainty and fear becomes a habit that is wired in to our millions of networks of brain cells. The result? Negative thinking!

To counter that negative thinking, it helps to listen to positive self-talk messages instead of negative amygdala messages. In time, you can actually rewire the unnecessary fear out of your programs. You can still be *aware*, but you don't have to be afraid. Someone will always let you know if there's a saber-toothed tiger on the loose.

March 31

"I am always considerate. I care about others and it shows. I am understanding and mindful of other people's thoughts, beliefs, circumstances, and paths in life. No one has to remind me to walk in the shoes of others; I walk in their shoes every day. And because I do, I am always considerate."

April 1

"I never let myself over-stress or get upset with the unimportant things in life. I take life seriously, but never more seriously than it deserves to be taken. I stay practical, always keep my balance, make sure my vision of tomorrow is clear and strong, and let the small things pass."

April 2

"I don't have to have the last word to be happy. I don't have to win an argument to be strong. I don't have to make myself heard just to prove I have a point. I don't have to be right to prove I'm not wrong. I like who I am, I have endless quality and an incredible mind, and I don't have to prove it to anyone."

April 3

"I choose to wire unnecessary stress out of my brain and out of my life. I know that I control my thoughts. I can override any thought that doesn't belong, and each day I consciously choose thoughts that are peaceful, calming, positive, and helpful."

April 4

"When the wrong thought tries to step into my mind, I immediately repeat the self-talk that says, *'I am in control of what I think. I choose to think positive, believe in the best, see the unlimited opportunities in front of me, appreciate the day, and enjoy this moment.'*"

April 5

"I like to play. I love to have fun. I love to be happy in the moment and be open to the amazing, positive world all around me. I'm serious and practical when I need to be, but I never forget that there is another world where I am full of fun, truly alive, and in love with life, just around the corner."

April 6

"I am wealthy in so many ways. I have more in my life at this moment than many people have ever dreamed of having. So instead of starting each day worrying about what I'm missing, I begin my day with gratitude for what I have."

Self-Talk Tip #17
A Helpful History of Self-Talk

The idea of changing our lives by changing our self-talk is very old. The Bible suggested the idea of self-talk in Proverbs 23:7, *"As a man thinketh in his heart, so is he."* Romans 12:2 said it even more directly: *" . . . be transformed by the renewing of your mind."* But the idea of using positive self-talk techniques for consciously reprogramming our minds would wait more than two thousand years before it would be accepted as scientific fact.

In the mid 1950s, following the 1920s-era writings of French pharmacologist Emile Coué, pioneering self-help authors such as Napolean Hill, Dr. Norman Vincent Peale, Dr. Maxwell Maltz and others, began to bring the concepts of positive thinking and conscious "autosuggestion" to the attention of self-help followers.

It was not, however, until the 1980's that self-talk, as it is used today, began to be generally understood. When researchers, using computer imaging technology, were finally able to see into the living brain, their research showed that because of the brain's ability to rewire itself (neuroplasticity), *self-talk*, practiced in the right way, could actually restructure the individual's brain with new neural networks.

Neuroscientists and behavioral researchers found that new input to the brain, such as specially-worded self-talk, could rewire and change not only the brain's physical structure, but the individual's attitudes, actions, and results as well. We had discovered that our *thoughts* physically rewire our brains—and the science of self-talk was born.

April 7

"I like to live from both sides of my brain. From one side I get lines straight and figure things out. From the other side I feel the peace that sunsets create, and find the joys in my life. Both sides of my brain are part of who I am, and I practice using both of them every day."

April 8

"I practice letting go. When it's time to move on or move past something in my life that is not part of my future, I think it through, am always mindful of the consequences of what I do next, and if it's right to let it go, I let it go."

April 9

"I am kind, loving, and caring. In a world where kindness and caring for others can be overlooked by the demands of the day, I never forget what life is really about. In my world, life is about love, caring, and service to others. In the final moments of the life I'm living, I will know that a life of love, caring, and service to others was what I came here for in the first place."

April 10

"I choose to never compare my own accomplishments to the achievements of others. I choose, instead, to spend my time improving myself and finding ways I can do better, not so that I can rise above someone else, but so I can learn to rise above myself."

April 11

"I make every morning important. When I awake I always greet the day with gratitude for my life and appreciation for being here, this one day. Then I think about what I can do today to express my life in the most positive, helpful way, and make the world a better place because I am here, and get to live my life, this one day."

April 12

"I think for myself. I may listen to others, and measure what they say, but I determine for myself the truths of my life. Instead of following blindly, I think for myself. Instead of accepting what everyone else thinks or does, I think for myself. And when, each day, I take the next step into my future, I think for myself."

Self-Talk Tip #18
Is Your Brain Wired to *Succeed*?

What really makes the difference in our lives? Why are some people successful, and other people are not?

Research tells us that our brains become wired for success or failure. As we grew, each of us got programs from the world around us, and many of those programs became 'permanently' wired into our brains. Those programs (neural networks in our brain) determine every thought we think and every action we take—which leads, inevitably, to success or failure in anything we do.

Since we were born, each of our brains has been recording, storing, and wiring in programs we received from parents, teachers, friends, and the world around us. If we were fortunate, and our brains got wired with enough programs that are positive and healthy, we live our lives in a positive, healthy, successful way. If, on the other hand, we got too many of the wrong kind of programs, we end up struggling—or failing—because of the programs we got. (No one *intended* to wire us to fail, of course.)

If we receive too many of the wrong kinds of programs, we end up living with them and wishing things could be better—or we *change* them.

Fortunately, our brains were designed to help us get rid of programs we don't want. That's why we practice positive self-talk—so we can change our programs. And this time we're going to get them *right*.

April 13

"I dream big, but I'm also very practical. I set specific goals, I put my plans in writing, and I take each action step I need to take. I dream great dreams, but I also take every step I need to take to make my dreams come true."

April 14

"I find happiness when I begin my day with gratitude, find something that is meaningful or beautiful that I notice during the day, do something of value, and go to sleep knowing I helped someone else in some way that day."

April 15

"When I look at others, I choose to see their qualities in how they look, how they present themselves, and the glow of life around them. When I look for it, I always see the best in others. And when I look at my own self in the mirror, I do the exact same thing."

April 16

"When I stumble or stall, I don't wait for life to make things better, or for someone else to get me up and get me moving again. When I stall, I stand up and take one step forward. And then I take another step, and then another. Because I always keep moving, I am never stalled for long."

April 17

"When I'm having a conversation with someone, I don't have to be smarter than the other person, I don't have to be the one who's always right, and I don't have to 'win.' I just want to live up to my highest potential, learn everything I can, express myself well, and contribute something worthwhile to any conversation I'm a part of."

April 18

"I never say meaningless words just to be talking, or speak in empty thoughts or sentences. What I choose to say, counts, and other people know it. My conversation is not idle; my words are clear, thoughtful, meaningful, and worthy of the quality of character I am creating within me."

Self-Talk Tip #19
Positive Self-Talkers are Happier Than Negative Self-Talkers

It's no surprise that positive self-talkers are happier overall. Most people who practice positive self-talk are not only more successful, they're more aware of their achievements and they enjoy them more.

The reason? They practice seeing the possibilities and solutions instead of just seeing the odds against them. Instead of seeing problems as roadblocks, they see problems as a learning experience and a natural part of life. The net result is they create a combination of higher achievement and lower stress, which can make anyone happier.

Positive self-talkers are also happier because they *practice* being happy; it's part of the self-talk they often repeat to themselves. Happiness is not an accidental state of 'being,' happiness is an attitude, and attitude is a choice.

Does that mean you can be happier just by making the choice to be happier? Yes, it does! Your choice to be happy, along with the right self-talk, can turn almost any day into a better day.

April 19

"I slow life down by controlling the thoughts I think and the focus of my mind. I never allow the meaningless, high-speed chaos of the world around me to pull me into its race to nowhere. I stand quietly, outside of the rush, away from the noise, calmly focused on a precious moment in a beautiful day."

April 20

"I listen to the quiet voice within me that is wise, caring, understanding, and always there when I choose to listen. I go to a quiet place in my mind, ask my question in clear, simple words, and wait for an answer. When I ask my question, wait with patience, and listen carefully, the answer always comes"

April 21

"I choose to listen to the earliest dreams of my childhood, and the unlimited possibilities for the life that I saw in my youth. So I stop now, see clearly the person I wanted to be, and ask myself the question: Have I lived my dream? And if I haven't, could I still?"

April 22

"Each day my self-talk wires my brain with a picture of the person I will become tomorrow. If I am 'down' on me, my brain will believe it, wire it in, and pull me down. If I am 'up on me, my brain will be wired to help me succeed. The truth is, my tomorrow is up to me."

April 23

"I am a person of quality. I speak clearly, tell the truth, choose to be strong, and am a person of direction and goals. I am honest with myself and others, I have both dreams of unlimited potential and the humility to appreciate every blessing that comes to my life."

April 24

"I'm never uncaring or indifferent to others. People count in the smallest and biggest ways, and I let them know it. I look people in the eye, I acknowledge their presence, I show them respect, and I let them know I care. After all, I am one of them."

Self-Talk Tip #20
Taking Self-Talk to the Next Level

Years ago, when self-talk was first introduced, it was recorded on cassette tapes for people to listen to. Today, people who want to take self-talk to the next level listen to specially recorded digital self-talk programs that are streamed to their tablets and smartphones.

The reason people listen to self-talk is because of the role of *repetition* in rewiring the brain. The most important rule of neuroplasticity for rewiring the brain is repetition. (We still remember the words to songs we heard when we were kids, when all we did was hear them played in the background. We learn new self-talk in the same way.)

Recorded self-talk goes into depth to get to the heart of issues like weight-loss, self-esteem, relationships, stress, work, finances, etc. It rewires a broad group of programs in the brain that work together to create new attitudes and beliefs about the subject the listener is focusing on.

This kind of "super self-talk" is listened to daily, and it is clearly the daily repetition that does the trick; hearing self-talk repeated in this way forms new neural pathways that are imprinted in the brain. People listen while they're getting ready in the morning, or while they're driving in the car, or when they're at the office or around the house, or when they're going to sleep at night.

If you'd like to take self-talk to the next level, you can find a complete list of self-talk programs that are certified by the Self-Talk Institute at selftalkplus.com.

April 25

"I have good manners. I am courteous and respectful. I pay attention to others. I open the door for others, allow others to go first, always say 'please,' and 'thank you,' and wait my turn to speak. That's not being lower or less than others; that's a person of quality having good manners."

April 26

"I watch my old programs playing out in my mind, and I realize why I have had to work so hard in my life. In my old programs I see my own resistance to making changes in my life, my own unnecessary fears about my ability to survive and do well, and old programs that doubt the successes of my own future. They are all old, negative and unnecessary programs, and I choose to get rid of them. I no longer need them, and I will do much better without them."

April 27

"I know that the most important words I ever say, are the words I say to myself. So I make sure I give myself the right dreams, the right goals, the right direction, the right attitude, the right strength, and the thankfulness for what I achieve."

April 28

"I know that every thought I think, or message I get, can physically rewire my brain. So I never let anyone—without my approval—rewire my brain for me. That would include friends, family, work associates, television, social media, or any source of the messages I get. My programs are my choice, not theirs."

April 29

"When I think about quitting, or giving up on something important to me, and I know I should keep going, I take time to get my thinking right. I remember my purpose, I regain my focus, I choose to make things work, and I come back stronger than ever."

April 30

"I know that people who smile more, live more. When the smile on my face comes from within, knowing I'm working with purpose, having good goals, living each day in a positive way, and being thankful for the chance to be here, I'm creating the smile that helps my life work right."

Self-Talk Tip #21
Your Brain Can *"Delete"* Old Mental Programs You No Longer Want!

Does your brain, like a computer, have a delete button? Researchers have learned that in your brain, when you stop using an old program, you stop sending nutrition to that program's neural networks; you stop *feeding* it, and in time your brain will delete it.

Neuroscientists call this "pruning." Like the gardener who cuts out, or prunes, old rose branches to make way for new growth and more beautiful roses, the brain will get rid of pathways you're no longer using to make way for new pathways to form.

If you'd like to prune out old programs you no longer want, the best way we've found to deal with them is to replace them with new programs—new self-talk—which, with enough repetition, will eventually become the stronger programs and take over. When you stop using the old programs, they will lose their nutrition, and in time, your brain will prune them out. And beautiful new roses will grow.

May 1

"l almost never get angry. l choose instead to pause, give it time, think it through, reconsider the other person's point of view, and think into the future, beyond the problem, so l can see just how important or unimportant this problem really is."

May 2

"I make it a point to get along with others, even if their thinking and life are different from mine. I choose to work on my own life, and I refuse to spend a moment worrying unnecessarily about some else's."

May 3

"I take time to stop and smell the roses. I am mindful of my day, each day, and how many moments I would miss if I didn't practice slowing down, opening my eyes, seeing much more, listening for more, and catching the smallest details of my life, instead of letting them rush on by. While I'm here, I choose to be really here."

May 4

"I choose to be wise. Wisdom comes from learning from my experiences, thinking things through, always thinking before I speak, considering more points of view than my own, and never speaking without having something worthwhile to say. I choose to be wise, and it is a choice that helps me every day in many positive ways."

May 5

"I'm never lazy. I may take time for myself, sometimes do little or nothing for a time, and I get the rest and healthy replenishment that I need. But I know that focused thought and taking action improves my life, and I make sure I create plenty of positive thought and positive action to move me forward and upward to my greatest potential."

May 6

"I'm good at taking care of the present, but I also take time to practice looking far into the future. I may not control or direct everything that lies ahead, but the clearer the vision I create of my own future, the better I do at making it work."

Self-Talk Tip #22
The Right Self-Talk is never "Pollyanna Thinking"

Some people confuse positive self-talk with being "Pollyanna positive." The right self-talk is very positive, but the two kinds of thinking are very different.

Positive self-talkers always look for the best alternative, but they are also practical and realistic. Good self-talk takes into account being practical and having your feet firmly on solid ground. Being aware, being realistic, and being responsible, are hallmarks of good self-talk.

The Pollyanna thinker, on the other hand, instead of using self-talk that looks for and creates the right avenues to successes, may rely on hopeful thinking alone, without the discipline of the practical self-talk that creates a firm foundation for the optimism.

When you practice the right kind of self-talk, go ahead, be optimistic. Expect the best. The rest of your positive self-talk will also make sure you're doing everything it takes to get you there.

May 7

"It's not me, it's my programs. If it isn't working, it's not the way I was born to be; it's the programs I received or gave to myself. If I want to do something wonderful with my life, I can get rid of the programs that work against me, imagine the future I'd like to live, and go ahead and do it. The only thing that can stop me, is me."

May 8

"When it comes to my life, I don't need help from people who are pushing, pleading, coaxing, controlling, or demanding. I do best with people who are reassuring, helping, supporting, encouraging, and believing."

May 9

"I find beauty in my life every day. I look for it and I find it. I find something beautiful in the smallest moments, from a simple smile, to a morning sunrise, to the sound of a child's laughter. Because I look for it, I find beauty in my life every day in so many ways."

May 10

"I make sure I have balance in my life. When I keep things balanced, I'm adding very important leveling to my life. When it comes to balance in anything I do, whether it is work, play, the food I eat, how I spend my time, the friends I choose, the sleep I get, or the goals I set, I use the self-talk that says, *Everything has a right amount, and I always create the right amount of balance in my life.*'"

May 11

"I always treat people well. If I were the wisest, most understanding, caring person on Earth, I would never question how I should treat someone, no matter what; I would always treat them right. So when it comes to how I treat people, I choose to be the wisest, most understanding, caring person on Earth."

May 12

"How far can I see? I can see tomorrow, and see myself taking steps to reach my goals. How far can I see? I can see months and years from now, and see what I will have reached. How far can I see? I can see the future, and who I will become. How far can I see? I can see the stars."

Self-Talk Tip #23

7 Rules for Rewiring
Your Brain

If you'd like to wire your brain in a more positive way, research in the field of brain neuroplasticity has identified seven rules for getting the best results. They are:

1. Mindfulness
2. Choice
3. Intention
4. Focus
5. Repetition
6. Emotion
7. Belief

Research shows that the more you choose exactly what you want to achieve; the more you pay attention to your thoughts and focus on what you want your brain to record; the more often you repeat the same message; the stronger you feel about it; and the more you believe in the outcome, the stronger you will wire it in—and the greater the chance that you will make it happen.

May 13

"Most of the limits I see in front of me, are the limits I created for myself. Getting rid of my limits takes practice and the right self-talk, and I make sure my self-talk shows me what I *can* do, not what I cannot. Because I choose to see beyond my limits, my opportunities are expanding every day."

May 14

"I find the joy. I know that when I take the time to look for it and experience it, joy is all around me. And because I know joy is near, I don't just wait for it to come to me. I choose to look for the joy, I find the joy, and I feel the joy, every single day."

May 15

"I choose to think about my self-talk today, and be consciously aware of everything I think and say. Because I am mindful and aware, and because I'm making sure it's the right self-talk, I'm making today work great, and my future work even better."

May 16

"I know that being reliable is a choice, and I am always reliable. I am able to trust and rely on others, and they can trust me and rely on me. I choose to be trustworthy and dependable, and I am reliable, in every positive way."

May 17

"Because I have learned to be kind to myself, I am always able to be kind to others. I care about myself, and it shows, and how I treat others is always a reflection of how I feel about myself."

May 18

"I am never afraid to stand up for myself. I never argue needlessly, or put myself above others. But when it's time to take care of myself, I'm alway willing to be a champion of me."

Self-Talk Tip #24
Finding the Holy Grail of Personal Growth

The "holy grail" of personal growth has been an elusive goal for many people who wanted to make their lives better. Now, with the discovery that the brain rewires itself with the input we give it, we have found the answer we were looking for, and what we suspected to be true turned out to be scientific fact: if you want to change your outcome, change your input.

The latest research from the field of neuroscience is incredibly promising. You can get past the problems or inadequacies of your past and create the better, more amazing person you would like to be—and you don't have to hope for a miracle or wait for luck, to make it happen.

This time, science is on your side, and positive self-talk is the key. We have found the holy grail of personal growth: *You can rewire your brain.*

From *The Power of Neuroplasticity* by Shad Helmstetter, Ph.D.

May 19

"I believe in myself. I know that believing in me is a choice, so I choose to like who I am, be confident in my qualities, believe in my potential, and believe in the best outcome of anything that I do."

May 20

"Of all the roads I could walk, I choose to walk the road that helps others walk theirs."

May 21

"I choose to control unnecessary stress in my life by making sure that I practice good health habits, look at the brighter future beyond the problems of the moment, consciously bring myself to a quiet place of peace in my mind, and know that within me, all is well."

May 22

"Each night before I go to sleep, I ask myself the question: 'What did I learn today that will help me do better tomorrow?' When I do this, I keep myself aware of my personal growth, aware of my responsibility to myself, and aware of the endless opportunities to help me grow."

May 23

"I love happiness! I choose it, I create it, I find it, and I make sure it's a big part of my day. The more I practice being happy each day, the happier I am."

May 24

"I refuse to be negative. I'm a realist. I deal with life, and I let negative things go. Anything that drains my energy or my spirit is not healthy to hold on to, and I give it no space in my mind or in my life."

Self-Talk Tip #25
When You Listen to Self-Talk,
Here's How to Do It

If you want to learn new, positive self-talk faster, by listening to it, here's how to get the best results.

When you're getting started, it works best when you listen to the self-talk in the background, while you're doing something else. (Recorded self-talk sessions are usually from ten to twenty minutes in length.)

In the morning, play the self-talk *in the background* while you're getting ready. When you start your day with the right self-talk, you set up your day in the 'positive.'

Another time to listen is while you're doing something *physical*. Listen while you're walking, running, exercising, doing yoga, or working out. Listening while you're doing something physical is based on research that shows that our brains wire better or faster when we're physically active.

Another good time to listen to self-talk is just before you go to sleep at night. This is a great way to end the day, see yourself at your best, and get ready to take on tomorrow.

Repeat the self-talk session each day for one to three weeks on any self-talk subject you want to work on. This will give your brain the time it needs to begin wiring in the new programs you're listening to.

www.selftalkplus.com

May 25

"My attitude is my business, and what I do with it is up to me. My attitude, my mood, and my outlook on life are mine to choose, and no one else has the right to choose them for me. No matter where I am, what I'm doing, or who I'm with, my attitude is my choice, and it's always up to me."

May 26

"I keep the positive child within me alive and well. I am curious; I am interested in everything. I find life full of exciting ideas and opportunities. I'm always learning something new. I have endless dreams about my tomorrows, and I can't wait for the next day to come."

May 27

"I take the time to listen to the positive ideas I learn from others. I find good ideas everywhere. I look for ideas that increase my knowledge, my skills, and my awareness. I am open to new ideas. I learn from them, and my life always gets better because of them."

May 28

"I practice using positive self-talk every day. Because I do, I have better days, I am happier, I think better, my attitude is brighter, I deal with problems and move past them, and I open my mind to wonderful things to come!"

May 29

"When I have a problem that I think I cannot solve, I remind myself that I can. I learn everything I can learn about the problem, think it through carefully, do my best to be very objective, make a list of the possible solutions, write a list of the steps I will take to overcome the problem, and take the first step."

May 30

"I will never stop dreaming. I choose to dream of the amazing, unlimited possibilities in front of me. When I take the limits off, open my mind to endless possibilities, and begin to imagine myself already being there, I am, today, creating the future that one day will be mine."

May 31

"Today I choose to find at least one thing to be thankful for, one thing to be happy about, one thing that helps me grow, one thing to look forward to, and at least one thing to do that helps someone else."

Self-Talk Tip #26
Why Do People Who Practice Positive Self-Talk Do *Better?*

Over all, people who think in a positive, optimistic way, and who actively practice using positive self-talk, tend to do better in dealing with problems than people who are negative. Why is that?

The answer is based on neuroscience. Thinking negatively shuts down the creative, open-minded qualities of the brain. Positive "self-talkers" are open to more alternatives, so they have more choices when it comes to solving problems and dealing with life. They literally see more solutions than people whose horizons are limited by negative thinking.

Neurologically speaking, positive self-talk 'wires in' the idea of giving yourself more choices, and being willing to see the possibility of succeeding. While negative self-talk convinces you to stop trying, practicing positive self-talk keeps you looking for a more successful outcome, until the right solution can be found.

June 1

"I am able to forgive and forget. I never spend my time being angry, holding a grudge, or adding any negative energy to my life. My brain is busy recording everything I think and feel, and I make sure my brain is recording love, forgiveness, and understanding. And what my brain records most is who I am becoming."

June 2

"When I have a job to do that might seem difficult or uninteresting to me, I change the job by changing the way I think about it. By seeing the job in a positive way, I feel good about putting myself into action, and getting the job done."

June 3

"I deal with fear by taking action or dismissing it. If the fear is something real that I need to deal with, I decide what to do next, and I take action. If the fear is something I should ignore, I dismiss it, put it out of my mind, and immediately replace it with something positive."

June 4

"People like me. They don't see the flaws I have imagined that I have; they see the qualities I have that make me who I am. And when people like me, I don't question it, wonder about it, or think it isn't true. I just accept it: People like me."

June 5

"I notice some of the smallest things in my life. I pay attention to things that, before, I may never have been aware of, in what I hear, what I see, and everything I sense around me. By practicing bringing the details of my world into focus, I keep my mind clear, sharp, alert, and aware."

June 6

"I create quiet in my mind. No matter what is going on around me, I practice going within myself to find that special place of peace, harmony and quiet. And from that stillness comes strength, understanding, clarity, and balance. When I practice creating quiet in my mind, I create balance in my life."

Self-Talk Tip #27
The Gold-Colored Brain

Imagine that you have a simple outline sketch of your brain. You also have three colored pens with colored ink. One pen has gray ink, one pen is neutral, and one pen has gold ink.

Imagine that every time you have a thought of any kind, you make a small mark on the picture of your brain.

If your thought is a *neutral* thought, neither positive nor negative, you make a mark on the picture of your brain with the neutral colored pen.

If it's a *negative* thought, you make a mark with the gray, dark colored pen.

If it's a *positive* or healthy thought, you mark the picture of your brain with the bright, gold colored pen.

Imagine doing that with every thought you think each day. (It's estimated that we think as many as 12,500 to 70,000 thoughts in a day, so that would be a lot of colored marks!) At the end of just one day, what color would your brain picture be? Would it be mostly bright and gold, filled with positive; would it be neutral; or would it be gray and dark, and mostly negative?

What would the picture of your brain look like at the end of a year?

And the most important question is: What color will your brain picture be at the end of your life?

From *The Power of Neuroplasticity* by Shad Helmstetter, Ph.D.

June 7

"I am stronger than the problem. No matter what it is I face, I know that I have the strength to stand up to it and the determination to overcome it. So I deal with it, and I move past it."

June 8

"I see life as more than the world I live in each day. I see life as learning great lessons, filled with opportunities for joy, the chance to learn to love myself and to truly love others, and the time for me to become the person I was intended to be."

June 9

"I have courage. There are times I may be uncertain or afraid, but because I choose to have courage, I replace my doubts with determination, and I change my fear to faith. And that creates my victories."

June 10

"l have respect. l respect others, their time, their accomplishments, and their point of view. l also respect myself. And because l like who l am and respect who l am, other people respect me, too."

June 11

"I don't avoid the challenge, I face it. I don't fear the new, I embrace it. I don't mind the work, I enjoy it. And I don't dread the day, I thank it."

June 12

"I have self-discipline. When I need to be in control of my attitude, my thoughts, my words, my actions, or my day, I have the right self-talk, and positive self-discipline to be in control of myself, and everything I think or do."

Self-Talk Tip #28
Is Changing Your Programs
Really That Simple?

Changing your programs may be simple, but it isn't always easy. As we've learned, what we call 'programs' are actually complex neural circuits that are physically wired into our brains. They're real, they are physically there, and they aren't going to change or go away just because we want them to. Thinking we can think them away doesn't help. Telling ourselves we're going to suddenly turn over a new leaf doesn't work. Wishing them away is just wishful thinking.

Our old programs got wired into our brains through repetition. And it will take repetition to replace them. So the solution, repetition, may be simple, but actually doing it requires some discipline and some action.

Reading the self-talk and the tips in these pages is a good way to start. Also, practice every day. Consciously practicing the right kind of self-talk creates awareness, and awareness, in turn, creates mindfulness—which reminds you to keep practicing. If you're listening to recorded self-talk, listen to it every day, and that will add tons of repetition to your process.

It will all get down to this: The more you give your brain repeated self-talk messages of the right kind, the faster and stronger those programs will get wired in, replace the old programs, and create the new self-talk habit. When that happens, the 'successful you' may look back and say, "Nothing to it. It really wasn't difficult, after all."

June 13

"I take pride in who I am, how I think, and what I do. I am never conceited and I never have false pride, but I take honest, healthy pride in my choices to be a quality person and live a quality life. And I am proud of the person I have chosen to be."

June 14

"I have compassion. I care deeply about people, their lives, and so many things in this life that need our love and understanding. I know that true compassion is expressed without the expectation of reward. But because I feel and care deeply, my life is immeasurably richer."

June 15

"I love to laugh. I have a great sense of humor. Part of life is a comedy, so I see life's little missteps for what they really are, and I enjoy every moment of laughter they bring. I love to laugh. It's healthy, it makes me happy, and it's something I do every day."

June 16

"I have focus. I practice paying attention to one thing at a time, and giving it my full attention. Because I have focus, I'm able to put all of my mental energy into anything I choose that's important to me, and I practice improving my focus every day."

June 17

"I'm a great communicator. I express myself well. I take the time to know what I'm thinking. I get a clear picture of my thoughts in my mind. And I express my thoughts and words clearly and simply, so I am always understood."

June 18

"I keep my feelings and emotions in check. There are many things I feel strongly about, and I show it. But I also make sure that I am in control of my emotions, and they are never in control of me."

Self-Talk Tip #29
Your Destiny Is in Your Self-Talk, Not Your Genes

Scientists used to believe that almost everything about us was set—cast in stone by our genes. But now researchers have learned that your DNA is actually more like a blueprint, with control switches that are turned on or off by your experiences. And that includes your *thoughts*. Your own thoughts can actually influence which of your DNA switches are activated and which aren't.

What the research suggests is that we may have far more control over our destinies than previously was taught. It was long believed that, although we weren't an exact carbon copy of our parents, the die was cast and there was little we could do about it.

In one way or another, our genes would determine our intelligence, our talents, and perhaps even how we looked at life. That would mean our potential as individuals would be the result of the genes we got.

It now appears that your self-talk may be one of the biggest factors in which of your DNA switches are turned off or turned on. The old adage that "the apple doesn't fall far from the tree" is *not* set. The exciting truth is, your destiny, who you become, and what you make of the life you've been given, is actually up to *you*—and the self-talk that directs your life.

June 19

"I'm good at dealing with conflict. I don't create conflict or seek it out, but when conflict comes my way, I immediately focus my mind on resolving it in the most positive possible way. I understand it, I deal with it, and I do everything I need to do to resolve it."

June 20

"I'm fun to be around, fun to know, and fun to be with. That's because along with being genuinely interested in others, I practice finding the joy, having a great sense of humor, and living on the good-natured side of life."

June 21

"I am very creative. I practice seeing things in new and different ways. I find alternatives and look for new solutions to any problem or opportunity. Being creative gives me unlimited chances to grow, learn, and make life a joyous place to be."

June 22

"I have vision. I see life beyond the moment, beyond the day, and into a future of endless possibilities. Because every day I practice having unlimited vision in anything I think or do, I am literally creating an unlimited future in front of me."

June 23

"I make good decisions. I think about my choices with intention, focus, and clarity. I think about what is right, what is best—both for me and for others—what the goal is, and what my intuition tells me. I study my choices, and I make good decisions."

June 24

"I am determined. When I have a goal and I'm doing what I know is right, I refuse to stop, give up, or give in. When I have an objective that is worthy of me and worthy of being fulfilled, I keep going until I reach it."

Self-Talk Tip #30
Things You Can Do Now to
Grow New Brain Cells

Would you like to grow more healthy new brain cells? Research has shown that some activities are better than others at keeping your brain cells active and growing. There are some activities that help you increase your usable intelligence or help your brain process information faster, while other activities help your brain get closer to staying 'forever young.'

Here are some tips that will help you find the right brain-building activities. Look for activities that:

- Make you think hard
- Require your absolute focus and attention
- Make you think differently
- Are repeated activities
- Tie physical activity together with mental activity
- Have a goal that's hard to reach
- Are something you can always get better at doing

With any activity you choose that fits these requirements, the self-talk you use while you're practicing the activity will be important, and will make a big difference in how well it works for you.

Whether the activities you choose include such things as practicing archery, learning a new language, learning to play the piano, or becoming comfortable speaking in public, the more you work at it, the more new brain cells you'll create.

June 25

"I focus on the job at hand, but I also focus on the results I'm creating. With any activity, job, or task, I look ahead and imagine the end results of my activity. The more I visualize the benefits I'm creating, the more energy I put into the job at hand."

June 26

"I'm very likable. I have a long list of positive qualities, and there are a lot of things about me to like. Right now, as I think about this, I mentally go over my list of things about me that people like. If I ever wonder about myself, I just go over my list of 'likables,' and once again, I feel great."

June 27

"I'm good at overcoming adversity. No matter what the problem or challenge may be, I am determined to deal with it, overcome it, get past it, learn from it, and do better because of it."

June 28

"I have no habits that are harmful to me in any way. I get rid of any habit that could harm me, and keep those habits that build me up and improve my life. I choose to be positive and healthy, in every area of my life."

June 29

"I don't just plan to do great and incredible things with my life, I choose to create them and make them happen. I work at living a quality life, I think about what I want to accomplish, and I make sure I grow and improve in some way every day."

June 30

"I am strong, capable, and willing to do what I need to do to make my life work. I care about others, and they help me in many ways, but when it gets down to it, my success, in anything I do, is up to me. And I choose to go for it, own my success, and make my life work."

Self-Talk Tip #31
Extra Help for Practicing Self-Talk

When you're practicing positive self-talk, here's something that will help.

One of the benefits of reading positive self-talk every day is that it gives you a pattern to follow—a style of self-talk you can adapt and apply to your everyday life. Good self-talk is a habit that will come with practice, and paying close attention to the self-talk messages you're reading each day will help.

Each time an opportunity comes up—and there will be many of them—practice rephrasing your thoughts, and what you say out loud to others, with the same kinds of word and phrases you read here. Every situation is different, but with practice you'll find that you're not only *talking* more positively in general, you'll also find yourself *thinking* that way, even when you're not focused on being positive.

Self-talk phrases like *"I choose to make today an incredible day,"* or *"I'm on top, in tune, in touch, and going for it,"* become more than words on a page; they become a way to pattern the rest of your thoughts throughout the day.

The goal, as a positive self-talker, is to be mindful of all of your thoughts, and consciously aware of the importance of your self-talk. The self-talk passages you read here can inspire a lot of good ideas, and, when you're getting started, they'll give you a helpful pattern to follow.

July 1

"When it comes to creating my best possible future, I have patience. I am willing to work for, and wait for, the positive results of my efforts to come into my life. I think ahead, plan ahead, and stay with it. And I'm willing to be patient and wait for the results."

July 2

"When someone says "I cannot," I answer "Why not?" When someone says "It's impossible," I answer that nothing is any more impossible than I believe it to be. And today, with my incredible attitude and positive self-talk working for me, anything good is possible."

July 3

"There is nothing that can stop me or hold me back from my own success and my unlimited future. When it comes to my future, what counts most is me, and the next choice I make."

July 4

"I take the time to appreciate the many blessings and the wonderful opportunities I am given each day. I may get busy taking care of the day at hand, but I am never too busy to be thankful for what I have."

July 5

"I consciously create peace, calm, and quiet contentment in my life. During each day, I practice stopping for a moment, take a few slow, deep breaths, recognize that I am on my journey, glad to be here, thankful for the moment, and at peace with my day and my life."

July 6

"I am always ready to forgive others, but I also remember to forgive myself. I'm not perfect, I'm still learning, so I expect the best and forgive the rest."

Self-Talk Tip #32

What Stops Us From Being That Amazing Person We Dreamed About Becoming?

When they're young, most people dream about doing something special with their lives. A lot of those early dreams *could* be reached, but they're not. What goes wrong?

Research tells us that most of our success is the result of the way our brains get "wired." Our beliefs about ourselves are the result of the wiring we get from others, and eventually from our own self-talk.

When we're young, and believe anything is possible, our brain hasn't yet been wired with what we *cannot* do. It just accepts us as being unlimited, with little or no disbelief to get in the way of our dreams.

But all too soon we're told—by people around us—what *won't* work and what we *can't* do, and our brain starts to wire those messages in as though they're *true*—even if they weren't really true when we first heard them. In time, many of those disbelieving messages become permanently wired into our once unlimited brains. And we replace our dreams with limitations. We could have done almost anything, but we got wired to do something less.

Thanks to positive self-talk we can change that. Because we can *change* our programs, and rewire our brains with the right self-talk, we can bring some of those old dreams back to life—or create new dreams that are just as good. And this time we won't let anyone take them away.

111

July 7

"I choose to create abundance in my life. Always healthy, always good, always more than I need, and always enough to share with others. With my attitude, the choices I make, and the actions I take, I create abundance in my life."

July 8

"When I see it in the right light, life is wonderful and beautiful. Today especially. That's what I choose. That's how I choose to see my day."

July 9

"I choose to make today an incredible day! I'm here, I've got everything I need to make today one of my best days ever, and I've got an entire world of positive opportunities in front of me!"

July 10

"Today I choose to be in a great mood all day, smile a lot, learn something new, uplift someone who needs encouragement, spend time improving myself, enjoy my day, and really like who I am."

July 11

"Problems don't bother me. When a challenge comes up that requires my attention, I take care of it. I focus on the problem, I study it, I make sure I understand it, I deal with it, I take the necessary action, and I move on."

July 12

"I make sure I'm headed in the right direction. I keep looking forward and I keep moving. I don't stop, doubt, or hesitate. I concentrate on the goal, keep my focus, stay positive, take action, and make every day count."

Self-Talk Tip #33

Having a Talk with Yourself Can Change Your Day. It Can Also Rewire Your Brain.

Some people used to think that talking to yourself was a sign of mental illness. We now know that having a conversation with yourself can not only be *healthy*; it can literally rewire your brain and make it better.

The problem is, most of what we say when we talk to ourselves is the same old programming, usually negative, that we were used to giving ourselves in the past. Research shows that most of our unconscious programs are the negative kind. So out of habit we continue, unconsciously, wiring and rewiring ourselves in the same, negative way.

But now imagine changing that, and having an entirely *different* conversation with yourself—using positive self-talk—the kind of conversation that tells you what you *can* do, and what *will* work. Do that like you mean it, and you can actually feel the difference physically.

Of course, while your day will usually get better, it takes more than a few talks with yourself to rewire your brain, and repetition is the key. The more often you talk to yourself with the right self-talk, the better it works. And the more you begin to rewire your brain in the positive.

July 13

"Today I choose to believe in my dreams, focus my vision, set my sights, get a clear, bright picture of my most important goal, and take a giant step forward. Today is the day I grab my goal and go for it!"

July 14

"Any doubts l might have had about myself in the past, were nothing more than old programs that weren't true in the first place. Today l have faith, l have drive, l have determination, and l have belief. l can do this and l know l can."

July 15

"Today I know what I want. I have a clear picture of my goal. I replace my doubts with determination, conquer my fears with faith, stop putting off my own success, and take action now."

July 16

"Today and every day, l choose to use the gift of choice. Each day l choose how l will spend my time, what l will think, and even what my attitude will be. l know that life is a series of choices, and l choose to make my life work right. l choose to choose."

July 17

"I make sure that I take time for myself. I help others, and I love them and care about them, but I also care about me. I make sure that I rest, relax, and do the things that give me peace, restore my strength, and replenish my spirit."

July 18

"My whole world is in front of me today. I have countless opportunities. I have unlimited potential. I have an incredible attitude. I have non-stop belief. And I have *me*. It's a perfect day to love my life and go for it!"

Self-Talk Tip #34
3 Surprising Ways Self-Talk Changes Your Life

#1. When you practice the right self-talk, you set yourself up for a better future. Repeated self-talk forms new neural pathways in your brain. Those pathways form the blueprint on which your future ideas and actions will be based, and the results of those actions lead to your successes and accomplishments. Rule #1: *Your self-talk sets up your future.*

#2. Your self-talk changes how you see the world. When you're down, it's hard to believe anything can work right. When you're feeling your best, the world changes. You feel in control of your life—and when you're up, so are your successes. That's because how you see your day affects your day. Rule #2: *Your self-talk changes the world around you.*

#3. Your self-talk changes how *other* people see you. Think of a day when you were unstoppable, feeling great, and on top of the world. How did other people react to you? When your self-talk is on top, so are you. And that's how people treat you. Rule #3: *The world treats you like you treat yourself.*

July 19

"I never give up and I never give in. Instead of letting problems stop me or hold me back, I look forward to my future, I deal with the problem, and I keep moving!"

July 20

"I keep a clear picture of my goals in front of me at all times, and today especially. I see each of my goals. I believe in my ability to reach them. I take every action step I need to take. And I make sure I achieve them."

July 21

"I know that my attitude is entirely up to me. So I choose to keep my attitude up. Even when things seem down or difficult, I know the one thing I can always count on is my own bright, positive, winning attitude. No matter what, I keep my attitude up."

July 22

"Today I vote *'yes'* to success. I was born to succeed; That's how I think. That's what I do. That's how I live. And that's who I am. When it comes to success, I vote *Yes!*"

July 23

"When I want to accomplish something that's important to me, I give myself the self-talk that says, *'I have the dream. I have the goal. I have the faith. I have the drive. I have the determination. And I have what it takes to reach my goal.'*"

July 24

"I do everything I need to do, when I need to do it. I make sure I know what needs to be done. I have a practical action plan to follow. I schedule my time to take the time to get it done. And I do it."

Self-Talk Tip #35
Getting Used to 'The Super You'

When you first begin practicing positive self-talk, the way you express yourself could sound strange to the people who know you. People who are unfamiliar with self-talk may wonder what's up with you, or why you're talking that way. They're not used to 'the super you.'

If you make practicing self-talk a goal, and make it part of your life, you *will* sound different. Your words and your attitudes will make some people think you've gone through an unexpected change in your personality, when you've just gone through a change in your self-talk.

When you start practicing positive self-talk, some people will love it, and they'll support you. But some may not. (Seeing you become suddenly highly positive could worry family or friends who don't understand.)

The most important thing about changing your self-talk, however, is not what someone else thinks about it. Practicing positive self-talk is about what *you* want to achieve: your goals, your attitude, how you feel each day, and living up to the individual you choose to be.

When you change your self-talk, don't worry if it sounds strange, or what other people might think. Just keep doing it. The results will speak for themselves.

July 25

"Living up to my potential is up to me. Doing great is my choice. So I never underestimate my self or what I can do. When it comes to what I can accomplish, and the positive good I can achieve, I never count me *out*. I always count me *in*."

July 26

"I choose to share my time with people who choose to win. Together we can achieve any goal, reach the highest levels of success, change our lives, and help change the world for the better. So I've made the choice to surround myself with positive people who believe in success, and together we win."

July 27

"I know that I am responsible for creating the dreams I choose to live in my life, and I am responsible for making them come true. So I visualize the dreams, follow my plan, take the next step, and make my dreams happen."

July 28

"I keep myself motivated. Each day I visualize myself reaching my goals and living my dream. I know what I want to achieve, I take action, I work my plan, I stay with it, and I get things done. I am focused, filled with energy, and very, very motivated!"

July 29

"Today I choose to turn any doubts I've had into the powerful, positive self-talk that says, *'I believe in myself! I can do this, and I know I can!'*"

July 30

"I often thank the people around me for being who they are, and for making my life better in so many ways. I don't have to wait for a special occasion to thank them; I thank them often, just because I appreciate them for who they are."

July 31

"I know that at any time, on any day, I can choose my attitude. And if I'm really determined to have it, that's the attitude I will have. So I choose, right now, today, to have an attitude that is positive, focused, healthy, upbeat, successful, and going for it!"

Self-Talk Tip #36

Your Self-Talk Determines Your Attitude Each Day—and Your Lifelong Success

It's amazing how your self-talk, when you're consciously aware of it, can change your day. The secret of positive self-talkers is: you're going to go through the day anyway; but what you make of it is up to you. People who practice positive self-talk every day literally set themselves up for their days to go better.

How does your daily self-talk, day after day, affect your life-long success? That's just math. The right self-talk, practiced every day, multiplied by the next year, or five years, or ten, *is* going to make the difference between life being average and life being exceptional. Living up to your best, and getting the most from every single day, will always come down to how you talk to yourself, and how you program your brain every day along the way.

August 1

"Why would I put off a better future when I can start right now? Today I choose to take control of my life, decide what I want to do next, set my goals, put myself into action, and take a clear, strong step forward, into my own, incredible, unlimited, positive future."

August 2

"I live each day in the light of sharing, giving, helping, supporting, and service to others. I care about them as I care about me."

August 3

"How do I make life work best? I choose my self-talk, look for the good, help others, avoid negative habits, avoid negative people, smile a lot, think in a positive and practical way, and work every day to create a life of health, and success."

August 4

"When a challenging or difficult day comes to an end, l let it go. Instead of dwelling on the problems of the day, l focus on what l have learned, and my choice to have a better day tomorrow."

August 5

"I am mindful. Throughout each day I am consciously *aware of being aware*—of my attitude, my actions, my thoughts, and my words. Because I am mindful, I control the direction of my mind and the direction of my day.

August 6

"When it comes to my goals, the most important thing l can do is to believe in myself. l can set goals, be strong, and work hard, but if l want to succeed, l will have to make the choice to believe l can."

Self-Talk Tip #37
The Amazing Power
of *Mindfulness*

Being 'mindful' is the art of *being aware of being aware.* There's a good reason for getting good at it. We're not aware of what goes on in most of our brain. Over 90% of our choices are made without our being aware of why we're making them. Most of the brain is working entirely on its own—without our conscious input. (That's where most of our problems come from; our hidden, unconscious programs are in control of most of what we think and do—and most of our unconscious programs are negative.)

When you consciously practice being mindful, you become aware of what you're thinking, and why, and you take back control of your life from the 90% part of your brain that doesn't tell you what's going on. If you really want to be in control, you have to make being mindful the default, and you have to get good at it. Fortunately, with some practice, you can do that.

Since you're reading this book, it won't surprise you to know that one of the best ways to become mindful of what's going on in your brain is to practice using positive self-talk. When you practice talking to yourself in the most positive, self-directing way each day, you become more mindful of *everything* you're thinking. And being *mindful* is where a successful day begins.

August 7

"Of all the things I have, of all the things that are important to me, the one thing I can always count on is me—my heart, my mind, my faith, and my absolute determination to live my life in a positive way."

August 8

"I know that my brain is constantly 'rewiring' itself with every message it gets. Every input I get, from anyone or anywhere, *counts*. That's why I choose to spend my time with people who are positive, upbeat, believing, and going for it. What my mind hears most creates the person I will become."

August 9

"I like: reaching goals, being organized, staying productive, keeping fit, looking forward, learning new things, feeling great, staying positive, smiling a lot, doing my best, helping others, and always getting better. And every one of those things is up to me."

August 10

"The moment I begin to doubt, I think about the best outcome. The moment I fear, I feel the real strength I have within me. And the moment I think I'm not enough, I remember that I am not alone. With my faith and my undying belief, I am greater than anything that could come against me."

August 11

"I count! I add value to the world around me, the people in my life, and everything I do. I was not born to be 'average' or 'indifferent'; I was born to make a difference. My value as an individual, my thoughts, my feelings, my goals, my words, and my actions all count. And I prove it every day."

August 12

"I choose to be successful in some way every day. I see mistakes as learning, problems as opportunities, setbacks as starting points, and limitations as a chance to grow. Every new day is an open doorway to my unlimited future, and one more day to practice becoming the incredible me I was intended to be."

Self-Talk Tip #38

Can *Anyone* Make Positive Self-Talk Work?

Can anyone practice self-talk and make it work for them? The short answer is yes, anyone can do it; *we're all using self-talk all of the time*—it's just that we're not always using the right kind.

The problem is, using bad self-talk is a habit, and one that most people aren't aware of when they're doing it. And because they don't know they're doing it, they also don't know the harm it's doing them. Day after day, negative thought after negative thought, they're wiring negative attitudes and opinions into their brains. In time, the old adage becomes true: they become most what they think about most.

It's precisely the fact that we use self-talk without thinking about it or knowing that we're doing it, that proves anyone can do it. We're all self-talking already.

Practicing positive self-talk is doing what we've been doing all along, but this time changing the words—and getting it right. Doing that is a habit that can be learned. Once you know about positive self-talk, and how it works, you can practice it for yourself. And *anyone* can do it.

August 13

"I never allow negative people to darken my day. They have their life, I have mine. So I refuse to let anyone's negativity affect my day in any way. When I hear someone's *'negative,'* I automatically and immediately replace it with my own healthy, *'positive.'* I think right. I think positive. And because I do, my day works."

August 14

"I know that I have a limited number of hours and minutes to live up to my best each day. So today I choose to use my time in the best possible way. I plan it, I do it, I stay with it, I reach my goals, and I make today count."

August 15

"I manage my life by the thoughts I think. My day begins with my very first thought, I live with my thoughts throughout the day, and each day ends with the last thought I think. Every day is filled with the thoughts that control my life, and every one of them is mine. What I do with each of them is entirely up to me."

August 16

"I live each day with the absolute determination to live that day in the very best way. And when I go to sleep each night, I look forward with positive enthusiasm to a brand new day tomorrow."

August 17

"My mind does best when it is constantly stimulated and forced to tackle new obstacles in new ways, and is continually confronted with new ideas, new opportunities, and new possibilities. So I set new goals, love the challenge, and improve my mind."

August 18

"If I had just one day to do what I need to do, I would not stop, I would not wait, I would not fear, and I would not give up or give in. That is the way I see today. I know what I need to do, and I do it."

Self-Talk Tip #39
Self-Talk and Anger Management

Could your self-talk have anything to do with how often you get angry, or what sets you off?

The answer is a resounding *yes*. Most common anger management problems are the direct result of a brain that has been wired to jump first instead of think first.

If you get angry or upset easily, you're actually wiring your brain to work against you. Do this: Instead of wiring your brain to be angry, set a goal to practice being completely thoughtful, patient, calm and understanding for the next 21 days—and watch what happens.

If you do this faithfully, at every opportunity, your brain will actually begin to rewire itself. It will physically begin to change. Long lasting change will take more than just 21 days of practice, but your brain is *designed* to change with practice. Want proof? Try it. You could find that you're getting less angry, and getting angry less often.

August 19

"There has never been a better day than today to work for what I want to achieve. There has never been a better time than right now to take action. And there has never been a better moment than this one to let myself know I can do it."

August 20

"Who says I was born with purpose and potential? Who says I can be the incredible person I was meant to be? Who says I can reach any goal I set for myself? Who says I can be the winner I choose to be? Who says all that, and who believes it about me? I do!"

August 21

"I choose to create 'quiet time' in my life. Time for my thoughts, time for my dreams, time to be thankful, and time to create the amazing life I choose to live tomorrow. When I take time for myself, I'm not 'borrowing time' from something else, I'm creating the incredible future I have in front of me!"

August 22

"I choose to be determined, strong, resolute, and unstoppable. I have courage, strength, and conviction. I was born to succeed, and that's exactly what I choose to do. I have what it takes to make my life work, and right now, is a great time to prove it."

August 23

"I know that the only thing holding me back from living up to my true potential, is nothing more than fear. Fear of failure, fear of change, fear of what other people think, fear of the unknown, fear of inadequacy, fear of rejection, or any other fear I have. And I also know that all these fears are false."

August 24

"I know that the greater my focus, the greater my results. And the more I practice focusing on one thing at a time, the better I do."

Self-Talk Tip #40

How to Make the Day
a Better Day

The next time you have a bad day, or when it seems like nothing is going right, there is something you can do that will help.

Your *attitude* about what's happening, how you feel about anything, is never up to what's happening around you. What *tells* you how you feel about what's happening, is up to you and the attitude you *choose*.

So on the next "bad day" try this: Immediately give yourself positive self-talk that lets you know 1) You're okay, 2) You can get through this, 3) Life, overall, is going to go on—it usually does—and 4) Your attitude is up to you.

When the day looks bad, and some old negative programs are working against you, read a page or two of the self-talk in this book. If you listen to recorded self-talk, choose one of your favorite sessions and listen to it. When you do this, you'll actually be adjusting important chemicals in your brain. The more you read or listen to the right self-talk, the better your attitude will get, and life will once again become worthwhile, and not 'that bad.' And it can happen in just minutes.

When you switch to positive self-talk, not only will you look at things in a more positive light, you could feel even better than you did before the problem came up.

August 25

"I'm never afraid to dream. I believe in the best for my future; I dream it, I see it, I prepare for it, I work at it, I create it, and I make it happen. I choose to live up to the best of my dreams, and I choose to make my dreams come true."

August 26

I'm not here by accident, I'm here for a purpose. My number one goal each day is to become the me I was destined to be."

August 27

"It's not what I have, or how much I can get from the world, that counts the most. I measure my success by how much I learn, how much I love, how much I grow, and how much I give."

August 28

"I look for ways to improve myself every chance
I get. And because I listen, learn, search, study,
practice and apply, I always build, improve, achieve,
excel, overcome, and win."

August 29

*"I have faith. My spirit, my belief, and my personal strength are
alive and well within me. So I move ahead, believing in the most
positive possible outcome, and bravely take the next step forward
into my incredible future. I have faith, and I am not afraid to live
up to my highest calling."*

August 30

"Who am I? I am the very best of the person I choose
to be. What do I want? To reach every goal I set, in the
most healthy and positive way. Where am I going? Into
a future that is filled with the promise of my own
possibilities. How do I know? Because that's who I
choose to be."

August 31

"Each day I look at myself in the mirror, smile, nod my head 'Yes!,' and tell myself the self-talk that says, *'I choose to make today an incredible day in every way!'* And then, in everything I think and everything I do, I create it, I live it, and I make it happen."

Self-Talk Tip #41
Are Kids Getting the Best Possible Self-Talk?

Unless a child is growing up in a home where the adults are aware of positive self-talk and how to teach it, the child is going to get programs from parents, friends, teachers, television, video games, etc., with no one standing guard against the onslaught of negative programs that are all around them.

If you have kids at home, the solution is obvious. Make sure they're surrounded with positive self-talk. Practice it, talk about it, notice it, correct it, and reward it. You may not be able to change the programming your child is receiving at school or from friends, but you can override a lot of those often negative programs by making sure your kids get healthy positive programs at home.

As a parent, there may be no more important thing you can do for your kids' futures than to teach them positive self-talk. The more you use the right kind of self-talk at home, the more they'll pick it up, and begin to make those same positive messages a part of who they are.

There are specially recorded self-talk programs for both younger kids and older kids you can play at home that will help, at selftalkplus.com.

September 1

"Today I choose to be at my best and make my day work in every positive way. Today I'm completely in touch with who I am, what I want, and where I'm going. Today is a day I move my life forward. I know what I want to accomplish, I take action, I go for it, and I get it done!"

September 2

"Almost any problem I think I face right now, is not really a problem at all. Because I choose to deal with it, in not too long, it will be gone; in time, it will be forgotten. The moment I realize that, my life gets better."

September 3

"I never complain needlessly. It doesn't help, so I don't do it. I'm glad to be here and I'm busy making my life work. Instead of complaining, I choose to look for the best, think of the good, turn the negative into the positive, and add more energy and life to my day."

September 4

"My personal growth is important to me. I believe in doing everything I need to do to improve myself and make my life better. I choose to learn more, see farther, work smarter, rise higher, and achieve my best in every important area of my life."

September 5

"If I want to make something of myself, it's up to me. It's not other people's doubts that count; it's my belief in me. It's not the challenges I face each day; it's my determination to overcome them. It's not the lack of opportunities in front of me; it's my willingness to find them. My success is not up to the world around me, or up to someone else; my success is up to me."

September 6

"I choose to surround myself with success. I spend time with positive people who believe in me. I read books that enlighten me. I fill my life with messages that inspire me. I write, read, and reread goals that motivate me. I know I will become the person who is a reflection of the world that I allow to surround me most. And I choose to surround myself with success."

Self-Talk Tip #42
The Strongest Program
Always Wins

In the brain, the programs that are the strongest outweigh the other programs that aren't as strong.

That means that if your programs to eat that extra piece of chocolate cake are stronger than your programs to not eat it, the stronger program will win —and you'll eat the cake. But the opposite is also true.

If you have wired in to your brain, super strong, super healthy programs that help you make better, healthier decisions, then *those* programs will win, and you'll make the better choice.

The rule is, in the brain, the strongest programs always win. So the programs you wire in now, with positive self-talk—if you practice them so they grow into super programs—will literally help you overcome the temptation to fall off your diet, or deal with any problem you're working on.

Diet, income, work, relationships, family matters, self-esteem—whatever you're working on—the strongest programs you have wired into your brain will be the programs that win.

September 7

"I help people win. I choose to help, support, trust, encourage, and have faith in others. I believe in them, and I let them know it. Because I look for the best in others, I always find it. And because I do, they get even better."

September 8

"I choose, forever, to remove the fear that I might not 'measure up' to someone else. I never measure my life by the expectations of others. I live my life based on my own positive expectations to live each day in the very best way. And every day, I measure up to me."

September 9

"I take care of the things that matter most. I never ignore what needs my attention. Instead of worrying about the unimportant details of life, I focus my attention on the things that count."

September 10

"l am always attentive and considerate of others. But l make sure l notice, pay special attention to, listen fully, understand, appreciate, respect, and respond clearly, sincerely, and with my heart, to those l love and care about most."

September 11

"There is no problem I cannot conquer, there is no challenge I cannot overcome. I have been given every talent and ability I need to succeed in anything I choose to achieve. If I want to do it, I can do it. And if I want to make it happen in my life, making it happen is up to me."

September 12

"I know that the real secret to my success gets down to my perseverance, my undying persistence, and my absolute determination to reach my goal. So I start, I stay with it, and I keep going. And because I will not give up, I reach the goal. That's how I think, that's how I live, and that's how I win."

Self-Talk Tip #43
How is Your Self-Talk? Are You Getting it Right?

All of us talk to ourselves all of the time. Until we focus on our self-talk, we're usually not aware of it. Without really thinking about it, we're either carrying on a running conversation with ourselves, or we're telling ourselves something—and what we're saying may be more complaint than truth.

All of our self-talk, conscious or unconscious, is helping to wire or rewire our brains. And most of our self-talk is the negative kind. That can literally wire your brain in the wrong way—with negative self-talk—which is the #1 reason most people fail to reach their highest potential in life.

Most researchers on the subject agree that there are two main reasons why so many people get their self-talk wrong:

The first is that most people aren't aware that their self-talk physically wires the neural pathways in their brains that form their beliefs about everything. The second reason most people get their self-talk wrong is because science is just now showing them how to get it right.

The big positive in all of this is that once you know what self-talk is, and how it works, it isn't hard to get it right. When it comes to self-talk, practice makes perfect.

September 13

"Each day is another chance for me to restart my life—with promise, opportunity, and unlimited potential. No matter where I've been until now, I have the most important part of my life in front of me, and I'm just now getting started."

September 14

"My greatest joy comes to me from creating happiness and well-being in the lives of others. In anything I want to achieve, it's not just me that counts; it's how my life and what I do, affects the lives of others."

September 15

"I have, spirit, I have faith, and I am blessed in so many ways! I am filled with life, full of hope, and determined to live up to my greatest potential."

September 16

"Instead of just receiving, I choose to give. Instead of just giving, I choose to help. Instead of just helping, I choose to support. And instead of just supporting, I choose to believe."

September 17

"Today I choose to be strong, confident, sure of myself, and unafraid. I know what I'm going for. I have an incredible attitude. I know I can do it, get past the negatives, focus everything I do on the most positive outcome, and do it."

September 18

"If I had one day, one time, one moment, to live up to my best, take action, get things done, move forward and excel, I would do it. And as soon as I think the thought, I know the truth: Today is the day, this is the time, and right now is the moment."

Self-Talk Tip #44
More Than a Few Good Words

Positive self-talk is more than just saying a few kind words to yourself now and then. It's much more than that.

Positive self-talk is the best way we've ever found to rewire our brains with the right programs. Along with that, it's a way of getting rid of the wrong programs—the ones that continually work against us.

Practicing positive self-talk is also a way of living; it's an attitude you adopt that becomes an important part of who you are. It's a way of taking control of your life, who you are, how you think, the goals you set and how successful you are at reaching them.

As one definition puts it, self-talk is: "positive self-directed, neuron patterning, personal mind-brain programming."

We just call it self-talk.

September 19

"Each new day is a chance for me to live up to my dreams. What l want to do, l can do. What l want to achieve, l can achieve. And who l want to become, l can become. l choose to dream my dreams, set my goals, work hard, and make my dreams come true. That's what l choose to do, with each new day."

September 20

"I know that the secret to unlocking the doorway to my most positive future is my own self-talk and every thought I think each day. So I make sure that the messages I give to myself are filled with self-belief, self confidence, determination to succeed, and an absolute certainty that the best is yet to come."

September 21

"There is nothing that is possible that I cannot accomplish when I put my mind to it, and decide to do it. I am living a life of unlimited possibilities. And all I have to do is decide what I want to achieve, put myself into action, take the first step, then keep moving, and refuse to give up! That's how dreams come true."

September 22

"It is my right to raise myself up, to get better, and to improve myself in every way I can. People who refuse to grow do little for themselves, and less for the world around them. People who improve their lives in positive ways make the world better for everyone."

September 23

"I can't wait to go for it. Just imagine what I can do. My plans, my goals, my future, anything I choose— creating my freedom, sharing with others, working hard, getting things done, and feeling good about myself. I can't wait to make things happen. So today, I'm not waiting. Today I'm going for it!"

September 24

"I practice seeing myself as I most want to be. I see myself doing what I truly want to do. I see myself being healthy and in great shape. I see myself accomplishing great things. I see myself being at peace and happy with my life. The more I see myself that way, the more I create what I see."

Self-Talk Tip #45
Your Self-Talk Today, is Creating the Person You're Going to Become Tomorrow

Imagine what would happen if the way you talked to yourself today would create the person you'd meet in the mirror tomorrow. That's exactly what's happening, but many people aren't aware of it. You're wiring who you're going to be, in the future, into your brain right now.

Once you know this, you can change or improve who you'd like to become, and you can start the process by the thoughts you think.

Are you as happy as you'd like to be? Would you like to be smarter? Do you want to do better in your relationships? How about your job; are you the best you can be at what you do? What about your talents and skills? Are you living up to what you could have been, or have old programs convinced you you're not as good as you'd like to be? None of those things are accidents. They're the result of your programs. And programs can be changed.

The self-talk you practice today will create the 'you' you're going to become tomorrow. That means that most of life really isn't the result of blind luck or fate. It's up to the programs you create. And those programs are entirely up to you.

September 25

"I make good choices. I choose to be healthy and fit. I choose the right friends. I choose what I do with my time. I choose my goals, and I choose my direction. And I choose to do my best each day. I choose my attitude, I choose my self-talk and I choose how I think. Today and every day, I make good choices."

September 26

"I choose to make today a special day. My life is on target, I have a goal, I know what to do, I'm taking action, and I'm doing everything it takes to reach my goal. Today I use the self-talk that says, *'I'm on top, in tune, in touch, and going for it!'*"

September 27

"I was born with unlimited potential, so I choose to learn and continue to grow. I choose to live up to my unlimited promise. I choose to become the me I was intended to be."

September 28

"My life is good. The moment I think about it, I realize how true that is. I'm here, I'm alive, and I have unlimited possibilities in front of me. Every day I'm here is a blessing and an opportunity to live up to my best. Once again, starting today, my whole life is in front of me, and I know that my life is good."

September 29

"My attitude is always up to me. Whenever I feel down, I choose to change my attitude and get myself feeling up again. No matter what's happening in my life, I choose to think up, be positive, feel confident, and believe in the bright promise of my future. When I choose to have a winning attitude, my whole world changes for the better."

September 30

"I choose not to worry, or fear anything that tomorrow brings. I am strong, I am capable, and I am confident in my ability to anticipate, make plans, take the right action, and deal with anything that comes my way. I choose to believe in the best, and when I do, the best is what I get."

Self-Talk Tip #46
What is the Difference Between Positive Self-Talk and 'Affirmations'?

The terms "self-talk" and "affirmations" are sometimes used as synonyms for one another, but they're not the same. Affirmations are positive statements most often used in spiritual or holistic expressions such as *"I am one with the divine universe"* or *"I am guided to seek the greatest serenity in all things that I do."* They may be similar, in some ways, but they're not the same as self-talk as we're using it here.

Unlike affirmations, self-talk gets very specific, very clear, direct, and to the point: *"I get things done. I take action. I set clear, specific goals. I work at them, and I reach them."* Or, *"I get up at 6:15 each morning."*

Good self-talk messages are instructions to your brain, telling it exactly what you choose to do, with detailed action steps that put you in control. When it comes to the mental computer that runs your life, you don't give it affirmations, you give it directions. Conscious, positive self-talk messages are directions for your brain.

October 1

"I know that true success, in anything I do, will always come to me in direct proportion to my value and service to others. I treat others well in every way, and life does the same for me."

October 2

"I choose to believe. Along with my spiritual beliefs, and the faith I have in the promise of the future, the one belief I have that will always direct my life for the better is the belief I have in myself. When it comes to seeing the best in myself, I choose to believe."

October 3

"Today I choose to make my life work right. What I don't like, I change. What I can't change, I deal with and find a way to turn it into a positive. What I do like, I focus on, give it energy, and create more of it. Today, I make the choice to make my day an incredible day in every way."

October 4

*"It's my turn to stand; my time to shine. It's time to do what
I came here to do, and become the person I was destined to be.
So I gather my courage, fortify my strength, and step
forward with enthusiasm into my incredible future."*

October 5

"I have great value. I have exceptional worth. I have
many positive qualities. I have a reason for being, and
purpose in my life. I count, and I make a difference.
That's me. That's what I choose to accept. And that's
how I choose to be."

October 6

"Every day I learn something that helps me grow.
I know that just one idea, one good thought, one
possibility that comes my way, can change my life for
the better. So each day I look for every new idea and
every positive thought that will help me become the
winning person I have chosen to be."

Self-Talk Tip #47

Could Positive Self-Talk Help the World Get Better?

At one time, self-talk was practiced by only a few people interested in personal growth,, but the concept of positive self-talk has since become a phenomenon that is now practiced around the world.

While people are reading positive self-talk, listening to self-talk, and practicing self-talk daily, through the sponsorship of the Self-Talk Institute there are now Certified Self-Talk Trainers who conduct "Self-Talk for Success" seminars in the U.S. and internationally on subjects as varied as self-talk for weight-loss, self-talk for network marketers, or self-talk for personal success.

Today there are even special "Self-Talk Boot Camps™"for kids—self-talk training events for kids and teens, with specially trained youths teaching other youths how to change their self-talk to do better at home and in school, and in life.

The self-talk book, *What to Say When You Talk to Your Self*, long a popular best-seller in the U.S. and many other countries and languages, has recently expanded into Russian, Chinese, Indian, Turkish, and Arabic editions, signaling the strong international response to the concept of self-talk and the positive rewiring of the human brain—and proving the global concept of an idea whose time clearly has come. (Imagine the self-talk of *personal growth, peace,* and *understanding,* having a chance to catch on.)

Will positive self-talk change the world? It certainly could. For now it will be enough if it helps your life get better.

October 7

"Who am I, and what can I do? I am a non-stop, go-for-it, confident, upbeat, positive, self-believing, super-achieving, always caring, dream-sharing, uplifting, forward thinking, future-building, life-embracing, success-creating go-getter with unlimited potential and endless opportunities in front of me. That's who I am, and just watch what I can do!"

October 8

"Changing my day for the better, by thinking right, thinking up, and choosing to succeed, always works best with practice. So I practice looking at my life each day in the most positive, possible way. The more I practice, the better I get, and the more successful days I create."

October 9

"I don't complain, I fix it. I don't regret, I build. I don't fear, I get strong. I don't wait, I take action. And I don't stop, I begin."

October 10

"How do I make my life work? I care about others, I believe in myself, I make sure my attitude is always up, I believe in the future, I set clear goals, I'm willing to work for what I want, I always have faith, and at the end of each day, I always know what I want to accomplish tomorrow."

October 11

"I take the time to rest, relax, unwind, recharge, regroup, reassess, rethink, reset, and recommit. Then I refocus my thoughts, redouble my energy, put myself into action, hit the ground running, and go for my goal!"

October 12

"I'm so blessed, in so many ways. I see the morning sun, I see the people I care about, I see the day with its endless opportunities. I see all the chances I'm given to live up to my best. And every day I remember the words: 'I am so blessed, in so many ways!'"

Self-Talk Tip #48
You're Probably More Intelligent Than You Thought

There is a very good chance you're smarter than you think you are. Or, at least, you can be if you choose to be. In a few short years we won't even recognize the standard IQ tests we relied on in the past. (How could a single test, administered perhaps only once during your youth, accurately define the intelligence of a brain that changes constantly and literally rewires itself every day of your life?)

If, as we now know, your brain changes based on the input you give it, then it makes sense that if you give it the right, new input, your useable IQ will grow along with it. At a minimum, the ability to use your intelligence more effectively will grow.

The new understanding that your real IQ is not genetically set from birth gives you the opportunity to reset your own useable intelligence. With that knowledge, and knowing that your self-talk plays a vital role in reprogramming your brain, it makes sense to practice self-talk and other activities that improve your mental acuity. And that's an intelligent thing to do.

October 13

"I practice being mindful of my own thoughts by consciously asking myself the question, *'Why did I just think that thought?'* Practicing being mindful of my thoughts puts me in control of own self-talk, and my positive direction in life."

October 14

"Today is the day I decide to go for it. Today is the day I set the goal. Today is the day I make the choice to make it happen. Today is the day I put myself into action. Today is the day I do it."

October 15

"When I have doubts, when I'm unsure about what to do next, I always remember to focus on my goal. I review the steps I need to take, make the choice to take action, believe I can do it, and take the next step."

October 16

"I choose freedom. Freedom of thought, freedom of vision, freedom of purpose, and freedom of my dreams. With an unlimited mind, and my unstoppable spirit, a willingness to work for what I want, and the determination to stay with it, I know that I can achieve anything I choose."

October 17

"I practice being alert and aware. I notice everything, and appreciate even the smallest details that make up every moment. I see the colors, hear the sounds, and look for all of the interesting details that make up this moment of my life. The more I do this, the more alive I become."

October 18

"I choose to be in control of my emotions, especially the negative emotions of anger, hurt, guilt, blame and fear. I choose instead to practice having happiness, understanding, acceptance, confidence, and joy. And what I practice, is what I live."

Self-Talk Tip #49

With Positive Self-Talk, You Choose a Future that Works

So much of the story of positive self-talk is filled with hope. Here's an example:

Is it possible that you get to choose your future, and make it a future that works? According to research in neuroplasticity and self-talk, that's exactly what you get to do. It's not where you've been or what's happened in your life up to now that will write your future—it's what you choose to do next, and the self-talk you use that will get you there.

Many people go through their entire lives believing in the old programs that tell them their destinies are mostly set, and there is little they can do about it. They are taught to believe that luck and the whims of the world around them, are the most important determinants of what happens to them—as though they are pawns in a game of chance over which they have no control.

But breakthroughs in the field of neuroscience tell a different story. We now know that much of what happens *to* us is the result of programs in our brains that literally set us up for success or failure, in almost anything we do.

The result of the research is that we now know our futures are not solely up to the whims of the world around us. You get to choose a better tomorrow, make sure you have the mental programs that will take you there, and create a future that works.

October 19

"I live today for today. I learn from yesterday and I prepare for tomorrow, but today I focus on today, and I make every moment count. Now is the time, this is the moment, and today is the day. Today is the day that counts."

October 20

"To learn the habit of setting goals, I start with a small goal. I write it down. I set the date, list the obstacles, write the action steps, and start with the first step. Then I stay with it, and reach the goal."

October 21

"It's not where I came from, what I have done, what I have or don't have, the difficulties of my past, or what I missed out on, that counts the most. The one thing that counts the most is the attitude I choose to have right now, and what I choose to do next."

October 22

"I am good at not arguing when there can be no positive result. I'm smart, and I'm mindful of my thoughts, but I also consider the other person's point of view. Instead of arguing, I listen, state my position or keep quiet, and make the choice to move on to more positive things."

October 23

"I have decided to be my #1 *believer*. I know that people who make the choice to believe in themselves, always do better than those who don't. So every day I choose to believe in myself and work at improving myself in some way. Each day I do this, is a day that works."

October 24

"Every great book and every wise person who speaks of success, all tell me that my success will always get down to how much I believe in myself. If that's true, and I believe that it is, then my success in this life, and in this moment, is truly up to me."

Self-Talk Tip #50

Who or *What* is Really Doing Your Thinking For You?

Behavioral research suggests that over 90% of everything we think is an unconscious replay of the programs that are already wired into our brains. Many of those programs are false, negative programs, and most of them were put there by someone else.

How much of your thinking is really your own? Probably less than 10%. That is, until you begin consciously practicing positive self-talk, taking control of your own programming, and wiring your brain with the kinds of programs that *you* choose to put there.

When you practice positive self-talk, your thoughts will still come from programs that are wired into your brain. But this time *you* will be the one who is consciously wiring them in. This time they'll be the positive and helpful kind. And this time they'll be right.

October 25

"I know that people who have little belief in the future see life as difficult, filled with problems, without opportunity, and nowhere to go. But because I practice believing in myself and in my future, I know that my life is full of opportunities, I can achieve anything I choose, and I have everywhere to go."

October 26

"I remember the dreams I had of who I wanted to be, and the things I wanted to do with my life. No matter how much time has passed, and what has happened between then and now, I still choose to have my dreams, and I choose to bring my dreams to life."

October 27

"Today is another good day to practice patience. I have patience. I know that having patience is essential to success, and an important quality in my life. I practice having patience every day, in the smallest things and in the biggest things, every chance I get."

October 28

"I do well because I know what I want. I have a plan to follow. I know the steps to take. I take action. And I do every positive thing I need to do to get me there. Because I know what I want, follow my plan, and stay with it, I always reach my goal."

October 29

"I am grateful for all the good in my life, and I show it every day. I know that the more I expect, accept, and recognize the good that comes to me, the more good I create."

October 30

"It isn't only what I dream about that counts. If I want to make something happen, I also set a real goal. I write it down. I identify the obstacles, I write out the action steps, and I get started. My dreams count, but it's the goals I write down, and take action on, that makes them happen."

October 31

"This is the time, this is the place, and now is the moment. Today I choose to reset the goal, have the vision to see it, the faith to believe it, and the determination to achieve it."

Self-Talk Tip #51
The Powerful Practice of
'Editing' Your Self-Talk

One of the three key steps for changing your programs is 'editing' what you think and say. Editing your self-talk is extremely important, and once you get the hang of it, it isn't difficult to do. (For all three steps to changing your programs, see Self-Talk Tip #14.)

As an example, when you're about to say or think any negative self-talk like, *"I can't remember names,"* stop yourself! Don't say it. Instead, turn it around and say, *"I'm good at remembering names. I care about people, I notice them, and I remember their names."*

That may not be true the first time you say it. But keep in mind that positive self-talk messages are showing your brain how you *choose to be,* even if you're not there yet. It you stay with it, and continue to give yourself the correct new self-talk every time the opportunity comes up, in time you will have wired that new truth into your brain, and in practice it *will* be true.

Do the same with anything you think or say that could be working against you. Change *"I'm never on time,"* to the opposite: *"I'm always on time."* Change *"I just know it's going to be another one of those days,"* to *"It's going to be a great day, and I'm going to make it that way."* Instead of telling yourself *"It probably won't work anyway!"* turn it around and say *"I can make this work. I've got this one,"* and then make it work.

Enjoy editing your self-talk! With practice you'll get good at it. In time you'll believe it. It will be you, getting to know the real you that you were meant to be in the first place.

November 1

"I know that no matter what the problem is, there is always a solution. No matter what obstacle I may be facing, I choose to look for the solution, find the answer, decide what I need to do next, take the first step, and deal with it."

November 2

"Some things *I Don't:* I don't wait for someone else to tell me what to do. I don't complain. I don't stop when things get tough. I don't let the rest of the world decide my future for me. I don't believe that everyone else knows best. I don't live for the approval of someone else. I don't fear being different. I don't wait for anyone to motivate me to take action. I don't believe in negative thinking. And I don't, ever, listen to the negative opinions of others."

November 3

"I know that there are unlimited opportunities in front of me. I have more possibilities in my life right now than I can even imagine. So today I look for the positive, keep an open mind, expect the best, and get ready for incredible things to come."

November 4

"I've got it! I have the goal, I have the opportunity, I have the tools, I have the reason, and I have the belief from others and the trust in myself. So I choose, right now to make the choice to go for it and make it work!"

November 5

"I choose to spend my time with: people who believe in me; people who trust me; people who believe in my goals; people who support me in reaching my dreams; people who accept me for who I am; people who encourage me instead of criticizing me; people who see my true potential; people who build me up, even when things are down; and people who care about me as I care about them. Today and every day, those are the people I choose to have in my life."

November 6

"I never let the world outside of me have more importance than the world that lives within me. I know that my own thoughts, my own feelings, my own direction, and my own steps, will always be as important to me as the world I live in every day."

Self-Talk Tip #52
Better Self-Talk, Higher Goals

The goals you set, if they're realistic, can only be as high as your expectations. And what you expect is always determined by your programs. That means that your self-talk creates the limits you put on your goals. If you want to set greater goals, you have to have the right self-talk to back them up.

Why do some people set a goal to travel the world, and actually reach the goal, while other people set a goal for something far less, or set no goal at all? It's because the person who plans to travel the world actually *sees* himself or herself doing it. That person has recorded programs that see the world-traveling goal as possible and achievable. The person without the goal is the person without the belief.

When you start practicing positive self-talk, it's a good idea to take stock of your goals. Write them down, so you know what they are. Then, after you've practiced the right self-talk for a few months, review your goals again. This time you'll find yourself resetting them higher. By reprogramming your brain to recognize what you're really capable of, your belief in yourself and your belief in your goals will have increased.

What goals could you set? What could you be capable of achieving if your internal self was completely on your side? The right self-talk will let you know that you are capable of much more, and reaching far greater goals, than you might ever have imagined.

November 7

"I stand up for myself. I know who I am, I know what I want, I know what I believe in, and I refuse to let anyone else tell me how I should live my life, or do my breathing for me. I care about others, but I live my own life, and I stand up for myself."

November 8

"I often take the time to pause, think about who I am, and the path I follow, and ask myself if I am doing what I was meant to do. Then I get a good picture of where I choose to go next, adjust my course, and take the next step forward."

November 9

"Some of the qualities I admire most are: a great attitude; compassion for others; self-confidence; positive goals; belief in the future; a willingness to work; patience; and determination to succeed. Those are qualities I admire in others. Those are qualities that create success. And those are qualities I'm building in me."

November 10

"I never speak just because it's a habit, just to be talking, or just to be heard. I make sure that when I speak, what I say is thoughtful, worthwhile, and genuinely contributes to what is being said."

November 11

"I decide what I want, set a goal, work for it and reach it. I give to others, while I take care of myself. I live each day with joy and purpose. I work at becoming the incredible person I was born to be. And I create a life that works."

November 12

"I know that *procrastination* is a habit, and so is *getting things done* a habit. So I choose to create the clear, positive habit of doing what I need to do, and getting things done, on time and in the right way."

Self-Talk Tip #53
'Getting Physical' is Good
for Your Brain

You now have another reason to love exercising: Physical activity helps you grow healthy brain cells. Combining your self-talk practice with a good exercise program, such as aerobic activities, will actually help you wire your brain with healthy programs faster and stronger.

If you're on a treadmill or working out, instead of listening to music as a background to your exercise, listen to a session of your favorite recorded self-talk. Set a goal to do that for 10 to 20 minutes a day. Listen to the same subject each day for up to three weeks if it's something especially important that you're working on each day—weight loss, self-esteem, getting organized, etc.

When you combine the right exercise with the right self-talk, your brain's natural neuroplasticity gets an energy boost that improves connections between brain cells and enhances your brain's ability to wire in the positive new pictures of you that your new self-talk is creating.

If you're not listening to a recorded self-talk session while you're working out, you can still benefit by focusing on the positive self-talk you want to wire in. Either way, try replacing casual music listening, or a random, wandering mind while you're exercising, with strong, active, positive self-talk. When you come to the end of your session, you won't just have improved your body; you will have improved your brain.

November 13

"I never belittle or criticize others. I know that it takes exactly the same amount of time to build someone up as it does to tear them down. So instead of putting someone down, I build them up. Instead of adding to their doubts about themselves, I focus on the qualities they have that will help them live up to their best."

November 14

"I don't tell other people how to live their lives. I only offer my opinion when I'm asked for it, and even then, I give it carefully and positively."

November 15

"I know that what I believe about anything, is always based on the programs I have stored in my mind. I make sure that the programs I have are positive, show me my best, and always lead me in the right direction."

November 16

"I find time to listen in the stillness. I listen carefully to the whispers of my soul. I listen to the quiet voice deep within me that believes in me, and helps me walk along my path. And when I listen, it is clear to me that my life has a reason, with great value and purpose, and I am not alone."

November 17

"I never make fun of anyone for any reason. I am caring, considerate, and understanding, and everything I do or say is a reflection of my respectful and positive regard for others."

November 18

"I never listen to gossip, spread rumors, or spend my time questioning the lives of others. I have my own gardens to tend to, and I stay too busy working on myself and what I need to do about me, to spend a moment of my time worrying about someone else."

Self-Talk Tip #54

Surrounding Yourself
With Success

Your brain is being wired by the people you spend your time with most. They're not trying to do that, but they are. It's the way the brain works.

Your brain is designed to record and store the messages it receives most. When you spend time with someone, especially someone you listen to and talk with frequently, *their* programs, in time, become some of *your* programs. That's why life coaches recommend you surround yourself with people you would most like to be like. Their attitudes and beliefs—their programs—will rub off on you, and get wired in.

In the same way, if you're spending a lot of time with people whose attitudes and behaviors are negative, then those programs can just as easily get wired in to your brain. If you have friends who are negative, it doesn't mean you should immediately call them and tell them dinner is off, or you won't be seeing them any more. But when choosing your friends, consider carefully who you want to have programming your brain for you.

When we were kids, our parents tried to tell us what kinds of friends we should hang around with. According to neuroscience, and how the brain gets programmed, they were probably right.

November 19

"I never create problems with others. I always find ways to create calm and understanding. I never let hurt, controversy, or uncontrolled emotions become a habit in my life. I choose instead to create the habit of a positive, understanding attitude, and a peaceful, centered sense of self."

November 20

"I make sure that I add my own intention to anything I want to create in my life. I know that intention adds energy to my thoughts, and the more positive intention I bring to anything, the better I will do."

November 21

"I know that the right physical activity not only adds to my physical well-being, but also to my mental strength as well. I make sure I am physically active, and I do everything I need to do to keep myself in the best physical condition. And that helps me feel better and think better."

November 22

"If there was ever a time for me to live up to my best, this is it! I am smart, capable, determined, full of ideas, filled with enthusiasm, and ready to make it work. So I have made the choice to reset my goals, believe in myself, expect the best possible outcome, get started now, and go for it."

November 23

"I measure my success in life not in material achievements, but in the number of lives I affect in a positive way. When I help even one person do better, I'm also helping many others around them, who I may never know or see. My life always has greater value and worth when I help another life work better."

November 24

"One of the most important choices I make is the choice not to 'fear.' Instead of being fearful, hesitant, self-doubting or uncertain, I choose to be confident, determined, self-assured, and unafraid. I know that strength is a state of mind, and I choose to be strong."

Self-Talk Tip #55
Visualization Changes Your Brain

When you visualize something clearly, your brain sees it as real. So if you want to imprint something in your brain, such as a goal you want to achieve, visualizing a clear picture of you attaining that goal will actually help your brain make it happen.

In a famous Harvard study of two groups of volunteers practicing a five-finger piano exercise, at the end of a week of piano practice sessions, both groups of volunteers showed an increase in neuronal growth in a specific region in their brain's motor cortex. This neuronal growth was the direct result of practicing the piano exercise for a period of time each day.

Here's the interesting part: one of the groups of volunteers had practiced playing the piano *only in their imagination*—without touching a piano! And they achieved results that were similar to those who had physically practiced on real pianos. Their practiced *visualization*, by itself, caused the new neurons to grow.

When you're practicing positive self-talk, make sure you're also visualizing the results you want to achieve. The more often you clearly visualize your intended result, the more your brain will see it, believe it, wire it in, act on it, and make it happen.

From *The Power of Neuroplasticity* by Shad Helmstetter, Ph.D.

November 25

"When I talk about myself, at any time, I always speak in the positive. That's not being self-centered, self-serving, or egotistical in any way. That's me, defining myself as I truly choose to be. The more I speak the best of myself, the more I wire it into my brain, and the more I create it in my life."

November 26

"When I wonder if I can, I think of all those who did. When I think I could fail, I think of all those who tried. And when I wonder if I should, I think of all those who never had the chance."

November 27

"Expressing myself carefully and well is important to me. When I speak, I always make sure that what I have to say is something worth listening to."

November 28

"I can change how I feel, the direction of my day, how well I deal with anything that happens, what bothers me and what doesn't, how positive I am, how much enthusiasm I have, and how much I will accomplish today. All of that, I can change."

November 29

"I am thankful for today. I am grateful for so much, and I remember to appreciate it and show it every day. I know that the more I count my blessings and recognize the good that comes to me, the more of it I create in my life."

November 30

To keep me mindful of my higher calling, I ask myself the questions: 'Who am I?' 'Why am I here?' 'What is my task?' and *'Am I getting it done?'* In the answers I give, I find the best of myself."

Self-Talk Tip #56
Avoiding Negative Self-Talk
Is a Healthy, Positive Goal

Because the brain wires in and believes what you tell it most, negative self-talk can literally wire your brain to *create* failure.

When someone is extremely negative, and negative most of the time, the results in that person's life are obvious to everyone. Negative programs create negative beliefs. Negative beliefs create negative actions. And negative actions create failure.

But even when you're only negative now and then, those negative messages add up. In time, they can wire themselves 'permanently' into your brain. When enough of those negative neural pathways begin to connect with each other, your brain will, all by itself, begin to look for more, equally negative programs to reinforce those you've already given it, like building a new highway of negatives, a little at a time.

The best solution is to set a goal to avoid *all* unnecessary negative self-talk. Bad self-talk never helps, it's unhealthy, it's a waste of time, it gets you nowhere, and it keeps you from focusing on creating the *successes* you deserve. If it's negative it's time to get rid of it. And doing that is one of the most *positive* goals you can set.

December 1

"Every day I make sure I laugh often, feel good, do something creative, find a way to play, have fun, feel the joy, and keep the child in me alive and well."

December 2

"I choose to never live my life based on the negative opinions of others."

December 3

"The most important asset I have is my attitude. With a simple, self-directed change of mind, I can instantly alter how good or bad I feel, the direction of my day and how it will go for me, how well I will deal with anything that happens, what bothers me and what doesn't, how thankful I am, how much enthusiasm I have, and how other people will see me. And all of that will come from my attitude."

December 4

"When I make a mistake, I ask myself what I have learned, tell myself what I will do differently next time, and thank the mistake for giving me the opportunity to grow."

December 5

"I forgive myself. No matter how much I've stumbled, and the mistakes I've made, I forgive myself. It is when I learn to forgive myself that I truly begin to love myself. So today, and every day, I forgive myself."

December 6

"I never blame others for my missteps. I take responsibility for everything I do. When I've made a mistake, I accept it, I learn from it, and know I will do better the next chance I get."

Self-Talk Tip #57
Positive Self-Talk Can
Lower Your Stress

The next time you see stress coming, before it takes over your day, there's something you can do.

Stress is a product of your mind. You're not imagining it—it's very real—but your mind is creating it. That's good news, because if your mind is creating your stress, you can also tell your mind to *un*create it. Stress is a symptom of your attitudes being at odds with something that's happening in your life. The internal conflict creates an emotional response, and like a bad habit, stress steps in.

How you feel about something determines how you react or respond to it. And who is in charge of how you feel about anything? You are.

There is a self-talk solution: Your *programs* are the source of your stress, and you can override the programs that are causing the problem. If you want to defeat the stress, immediately create a new message to your brain:

"I had hoped it wouldn't rain today, but it's raining, somebody needs the rain, and I can live with it and still have a great day."

"I have a lot to do, but I'll do the very best I can. I'm thankful for the job, and glad to be doing it."

"I know that families sometimes argue, but I love my family and I know tomorrow will be a better day."

When your world is not entirely in your control, there is one thing you *can* control, and that is your attitude, and the stress that comes with it. And the one way you can always control your attitude is with the right self-talk.

December 7

"I'm a great listener! When someone is talking to me, I focus, pay attention, make eye contact, and instead of thinking what I'm going to say next, I listen to their words, and listen to the meaning beyond their words. When I speak, I speak well. But when I listen, I listen."

December 8

"Before I expect something from anyone else, I first expect something from myself. I choose to give first and expect last."

December 9

"It isn't life's problems that count the most. It's how I choose to deal with them, that counts. Problems may be challenges, but I choose to deal with each of them in the most positive possible way. I'm glad to be here, and problems are not a problem for me."

December 10

"Today I choose to look for the positive, practice smiling, do something healthy, learn something new, take some time for myself, and do something for someone else."

December 11

"If I can do it for others, I can do it for me. I take time for others; but I also take time for myself. I listen to what others have to say, but I also listen just as attentively to anything I have to say. I care about others, but I always remember to show myself that I truly care about me. I believe in others, and I let them know it; but I make sure to let myself know, that I also believe in me."

December 12

"In anything I do, I choose to create benefits for others. I win most when others win, too."

Self-Talk Tip #58

Self-Quiz: Are You a
Positive Self-Talker?

Whether you're just getting started as a positive self-talker, or you've been at it for years, here is a simple quiz that will tell you how well you're doing.

- How often do you notice your own self-talk during the day? Often___ Occasionally___ Almost never___
- Do you edit what you might have said or thought, and replace it with better self-talk?
- Instead of arguing or disagreeing, do you stop, think, and recognize the self-talk of the other person?
- Do you consciously work to improve your own self-talk?
- Do you see positive self-talk as a short-term idea for your personal growth, or do you see it as a life-long solution?
- Is everything you say, especially to yourself, stated in the healthiest, most positive, way?

You'll know just from answering those few questions how well you're doing at becoming a positive self-talker. Wherever you stand, just keep practicing the right self-talk. Doing that will create one of the most helpful habits you will ever have.

December 13

"If there's something that's holding me back, I don't just wait for it to go away. I figure out what it is, I take action, and I deal with it."

December 14

"Today I am unstoppable! I have my goal, I know what to do, and today I choose to do it! I am strong, upbeat, capable, clear-thinking, determined, smart, sure of myself, thinking positive, heading for the future, full of energy, filled with enthusiasm, ready to win, excited about my life, and ready to make it work!"

December 15

"I know that life is incredibly good, and filled with endless opportunities. So every day I look for the good, choose the best, and do every positive thing it takes to reach my goal. My success, in anything I do, is not an accident, it is a choice."

December 16

"I make sure I keep my balance and perspective. When things don't go my way, I let myself know that *I can deal with this, I will get past this, and tomorrow is another day.*"

December 17

"Who says I can't do it? Who says I can't reach my goal? Who says I don't get to live my dreams? If you want to know who I really am, just watch me. I reach my goals. I live up to my dreams, and I make them come true. That's who I am and that's what I do."

December 18

"It's great to feel that I have done well for myself. But I make sure I have also done well in adding to the lives of others, and always in a positive way."

Self-Talk Tip #59

A Year of Super Self-Talk

As one year starts to close and another year gets ready to begin, we often think forward, about what we could do next. Get a new job, learn a new language, find the right mate, take a trip, or do something we've been putting off doing. The list can be endless.

As you prepare to write your goals for the new year, be sure to put a number one, absolute, *must do*, at the top of your list: *"Become an expert positive self-talker."*

Of any goal you put on your list for the upcoming year, that one thing, changing your self-talk to help you excel, will do more to help you reach the other goals you set than anything else you could do.

Write this one down: "My goal is *to be an expert positive self-talker."*

With that one goal, you can change yourself in wonderful ways, change how you deal with anything that happens in your life, change or improve your attitude about everything, and change how you get to look at every single day of the year to come.

That's a goal worth reaching.

December 19

"Okay world, get ready! I'm here, I'm prepared, I'm filled with energy and enthusiasm, and I'm going for it! You might as well be on my side and help me get there, because with you or without you, I've made the positive choice to win!"

December 20

"I never let any of my 'limitations' stop me or hold me back. I know that I have the ability to reach any goal I set, and there is no limitation that can stand in the way of my success. After all, I created my limitations in the first place, and I can let them go."

December 21

"By creating the dream in my mind, I make it happen in my life. I follow the simple steps of: *dream, goal, plan, action, perseverance* and *achievement*. That's the way success works. That's the way I choose to make my life work."

December 22

"The more times I think the thought, the more I program the message in my mind, and the more I create it in my life. So I always think and repeat good, healthy, positive thoughts."

December 23

"In the midst of my dream, I remember my goal. In the midst of my goal, I remember my plan. In the midst of my plan, I remember my task. In the midst of my task, I remember my day. In the midst of my day, I remember the moment. And in the midst of the moment, I remember my dream."

December 24

"If I were a pauper, with no gift to give; if I were someone, with nothing to share; if I were a person with no way to help, I would give others the words that make life better in so many ways. Giving words like *hope, peace, caring, understanding, trust, faith, promise, belief,* and *love,* are gifts I choose to give every day."

Self-Talk Tip #60
Finding the Incredible You

As you read the positive self-talk messages in this book, there is something you should know about you: *You were born to achieve.*

You were born with unlimited promise and potential. No matter what has happened in your life up to now, the potential you were born with has never gone away. It may have gotten covered over for a time with the experiences and the difficulties of life, but the incredible person you were born to be *never* goes away.

Old, negative programs in the brain make us believe that we are not capable, not good enough, or smart enough, or talented enough, or destined enough—but all of those programs are wrong.

You have, today, everything you need to make your life work in an exceptional way. If you wonder if that's true, that's just the old, out-of-date, negative programs trying to convince you otherwise.

Do this: Practice positive self-talk. While you're practicing, ask yourself the question: *Would I like to be the person that my positive self-talk is showing me?*

If that's the person you want to be, and if you continue to talk to yourself in the most positive, believing way, your life is going to change. The change will be glorious and amazing. *You will be finding the incredible you you were born to be.* And you will have brought it all to life with your dreams, your belief, and your self-talk.

December 25

"When I ask myself the question, 'What am I doing with my life today?' I always know the answer. I am thinking up, being certain of who I am, sure of what I want, helping others, reaching my goals, and doing everything I need to do to make life work . . . today especially!"

December 26

"I choose to create balance in my life. Along with my goals and my determination to take action and make each day count, I also practice having patience, staying calm, creating serenity and peace of mind, and making my day a quality day in every way."

December 27

"I am creative. My only limits are those I accept for myself. When I think, I think positive and possible. When I dream, I dream fearlessly beyond. And when I *do*, I do those things that make my ideas come to life. I am creative, and I love creating good things."

December 28

"I am responsible for my place, my choices, and my direction in life. I know that what I make of myself, and what I make of my life, is up to me. So I set my course, I make good choices, I follow my path, and I take personal responsibility for every step I take along the way."

December 29

"The attitude I choose to have, day after day, will do more for me than anything else that happens each day. How I look at my life right now, today, and how I feel about it, is entirely up to my attitude— and my attitude is entirely up to me."

December 30

"It's not what I fear; it's what I have the courage to face. It's not what I've missed; it's what I have the vision to see. It's not what I cannot do; it's what I'm willing to achieve. It's not who I'm not; it's who I choose to be."

December 31

"Instead of making New Years resolutions, I set clear, specific goals. I write each goal down on paper, along with the date I intend to reach it. I list the obstacles to reaching the goal. I then write the action steps I'll take to deal with each obstacle. I take action on each step. I review my goals for five minutes every morning. And I reach my goals."

You are invited to join Self-Talk+Plus™

If you would like to join an online community of positive self-talkers—people like you who are working to make their lives better—you are invited to join Self-Talk+Plus™. This is the inspiring online community where members stream self-talk to their smartphones, get to know each other, join in online activities, receive help from experienced life coaches, and share ideas that help them reach their goals. To visit this amazing online community go to **selftalkplus.com**.

 Listen to Certified Self-Talk Programs™ on your tablet or smartphone today at selftalkplus.com.

Made in the USA
Columbia, SC
04 February 2021

✦ ✦

About the Contributors

Warren Bennis is Distinguished Professor of Business Administration and founding chairman of the Leadership Institute at the University of Southern California. He has held senior academic positions at several other universities, including MIT, Harvard, and INSEAD, and has consulted for many companies. As an author or editor, Dr. Bennis has produced over 900 articles and 20 books, the most recent being *An Invented Life: Reflections on Leadership and Change* (1994).

John Child is the Guinness Professor of Management Studies at the Judge Institute of Management Studies, University of Cambridge, and editor-in-chief of *Organization Studies*. Previously, he was dean and director of the European Community's Management Institute in China. He is advisor to leading companies, with particular attention to the management of foreign ventures in China. An author of many books, his most recent publication is *Management in China During the Age of Reform* (1994).

Peter F. Drucker has been writing on management since he published *The Future of Industrial Man*—his second book—in 1943. A frequent contributor to the *Harvard Business Review*, he has since 1971 been Professor of Social Science & Management at The Claremont Graduate School in Claremont, California. His latest book is *Post Capitalist Society* (1993).

Angela Dumas is an assistant professor in Design Management and the Director of the Centre for Design Management at the London

Business School. She has published several papers on the integration of design into new product development teams and on the role of middle managers in that process. She is a fellow of both the Royal Society of Arts and the Chartered Society of Designers.

Tokihiko Enomoto is a professor of business administration at Tokai University, Japan. In 1986, he and several colleagues established The Mary Parker Follett Association of Japan. With Tadashi Mito, he wrote *Mary Parker Follett* (1986), a study of Follett's life and theories; he has also written several books about business administration based on the theories of Mary Parker Follett.

Pauline Graham is a lecturer and consultant on management and marketing. Formerly, she ran her own international accountancy practice and worked in general management in the retail trade. An authority on the management philosophy of Mary Parker Follett, she has written *Dynamic Managing—The Follett Way* (1987) and *Integrative Management—Creating Unity from Diversity* (1991).

Rosabeth Moss Kanter holds the Class of 1960 Chair as Professor of Business Administration at the Harvard Business School. Her many books include the best-selling, award-winning *When Giants Learn to Dance* and *The Change Masters*. An advisor to leading companies worldwide, she also served as editor of the *Harvard Business Review* from 1989 to 1992 and hosts "Rosabeth Moss Kanter on Synergies, Alliances, and New Ventures" in the Harvard Business School Video Series.

Paul R. Lawrence is the Wallace Brett Donham Professor of Organizational Behavior, Emeritus, at the Harvard Business School, where he served as chairman of the organizational behavior area and also as chairman of both the MBA and AMP programs. His most recent book, with A. Charalambos Vlachoutsicos, is *Behind the Factory Walls: Decision Making in Soviet and U.S. Enterprises* (Harvard Business School Press, 1990).

Henry Mintzberg is Bronfman Professor of Management at McGill University and former president of the Strategic Management Society. He is a two-time winner of the McKinsey Award for the best *Harvard Business Review* article, for "The Manager's Job: Folklore and Fact" (1975) and "Crafting Strategy" (1987). His most recent book is *The Rise and Fall of Strategic Planning* (1994).

Nitin Nohria is an associate professor in the organizational behavior/human resource management area at the Harvard Business School. With Robert G. Eccles, he is the co-author of *Networks and Organizations: Structure, Form, and Action* (1993) and *Beyond the Hype: Rediscovering the Essence of Management* (1994), both published by the Harvard Business School Press.

Sir Peter Parker is chairman of the London School of Economics. He has also been the chairman of British Rail, a member of the National Economic Development Council, a founding member of the Foundation for Management Education, and chairman of the British Institute of Management. He holds the RSA Gold Medal for Design as well as several honorary degrees. His autobiography, *For Starters—the business of life*, was published in 1989.